WINGSPAN:
Rising Above the Challenges of Single Parenting

MICAH LEYDORF

& CHRISTY STEWART

Blessings!
Micah Leydorf

DEDICATION

This book is dedicated to God—the author and finisher of all great stories—and the One who has given me the desires of my heart.—ML

And also to our precious husbands who often felt like single parents over the last nine months as we poured our hearts and souls into this book. Thank you Lou, Destiny, Moses, and Hannah, you inspire me every day.—CS

CONTENTS

FOREWORD
BY BEN NOCKLES
FOUNDER OF THE 111 PROJECT

I've heard it said "the most personal is the most universal, the most hidden is the most public, and the most solitary is the most communal."

Pause for a moment, if you will, to give consideration to this thought.

Does it seem counterintuitive? Most personal; most universal.

Does it resonate as good, right, and true? Most hidden; most public.

Does it stir something within you? Most solitary; most communal.

Does it bind you up or set you free?

My hope and intention in sharing this idea from the internationally renowned priest and author, respected professor, and beloved pastor Henri Nouwen is to present a truth that would liberate your mind and awaken your heart to the reality that YOU ARE NOT ALONE.

Throughout this book, you will find the stories and perspectives of men and women, moms and dads just like yourself who have walked this very same road (or perhaps some slight variation thereof).

"By giving words to these intimate experiences (the most personal, hidden, and solitary moments and seasons of life) they can make their life available to you" if only you'll let them.

And in so doing we can figuratively (and maybe literally someday over a long meal or nice and overpriced cup of coffee) look one another in the eyes and say with or without words:

"I know what it's like."

"I know how it feels."

"Me, too!"

So while I and the other contributors of this important work don't wish to project our experience onto you in some forceful and/or entirely unhelpful

i

fashion, my guess is that we share something (or a lot of somethings) in common.

But the first and most fundamental characteristic that we hold in common is not our single parenting per say, but rather out shared humanity.

And until we recognize this shared humanity we will be completely incapable of responding compassionately to one another.

You see, "compassion is not a relationship between the healer and the wounded. It's a relationship among equals (namely the wounded). Only when we know our own darkness well can we be present with the darkness of others."

The human experience guarantees some measure of suffering.

Jesus said, "In this world you will have trouble..."

Frederick Beuchner said, "Here is the world. Beautiful and terrible things will happen..."

My guess is that throughout the circumstances of life that have "forced" single parenting upon you, you have come to know and been made familiar with (these words come to mind):

-Pain, loss, stress, and tension;
-betrayal, abandonment;
-tough decisions and gut-wrenching choices;
-misunderstandings and utter disappointments;
-irreparable harm and all too costly mistakes;
-failure, regret, anger, and grief;
-shame, blame, trial, and hardship;
-heartache, anxiety, panic, and fear, etc.

I'm the first to admit that the above mentioned emotions, descriptions, and realities are far from pleasant.

We've been conditioned to distance ourselves from the discomforts of life.

We live in a culture of avoidance.

We've turned our back on the past—disowning our stories.

"The power of owning our stories, even (especially) the difficult ones, is that we get to (re)write the ending."

We must step into the brokenness of our lives, confronting and coming to terms with our frail and depraved condition, if ever we are to settle into our roles as a "wholehearted parent" (single or otherwise).

To become a healthy parent we must become a whole person.

"For parents this means we are called upon to acknowledge that we can't give our children (that which) we don't have and so we must let them share in our journey to grow, change, and learn" and in so doing "honor our children by continuing our own journeys toward Wholeheartedness."

"Wholehearted parenting is not having it all figured out and passing it down—it's learning and exploring together."

Brene Brown, Ph.D., LMSW, in her book *Daring Greatly* (from which much of the aforementioned quoted material comes and for which I highly recommend and strongly encourage you to read) said, "Like many of you, parenting (and single parenting I might add) is by far my boldest and most daring adventure."

But parenting is not merely a challenge to be met with new tactics and acquired skill-sets (as helpful as they may be); it is really the invitation to embark on a journey toward wholehearted living.

And who better to lead and show us the way on this "bold and daring adventure" we know of as parenting (and life) than our very own (wild-eyed, awestruck, strong-willed, meek-and-mild, joy-filled, thrill-seeking, ever-curious, always-playful, tenderhearted, soft-spoken, loudmouthed, plain-Jane, wallflower, devilishly-cute, drop-dead-gorgeous, heartbreaker, grow-up-way-too-fast, on-and-on-I-could-go, you-fill-in-the-blanks) children.

Me Too,

Benjamin Nockels

Micah Leydorf & Christy Stewart

PREFACE –

MICAH'S STORY

I have a secret. I've always wanted to write a book. Always. From the time I was in elementary school filling up a pink lined journal with stories of horses with my best friend to junior high passing notes with short stories that had surprise endings, I've always dreamed of being a writer. Nothing seemed more glamorous, more meaningful, more significant.

I've never wanted to be a pilot, a model, the president, but I've always wanted to be a teller of stories. But even as a junior high school girl, I knew it was unrealistic. Surely, everyone else wanted the rare privilege of telling stories as well. Not everyone could be a writer, so why should I with talents so very mediocre, be so blessed?

So just as I outgrew my obsession with horses and no longer passed notes in class, I traded writing short stories for my friends for a masters degree in journalism and the more sensible world of drafting press releases and op-eds on Capitol Hill. Then I became a mother, and everything else faded to background.

Seven years later, I went to a Bible study—on organization of all things. The book we were reading claimed that God gives us all a passion. It stated that our passion doesn't change with the years, that God gave it to us for a reason, and that we have a responsibility to use it.

Those simple words stirred the embers lying long dormant in my soul, a desire I had pushed aside as juvenile delusions. Immediately I knew my passion was writing, that it always had been, that it would never change. Those words freed me. Not only did I have permission, but I had a responsibility to use what God had given me. I had always thought indulging my passion would be selfish—irresponsible even. Instead, I suddenly realized that like the steward in the biblical parable, I had buried the portion he had entrusted me with (small as it may be) instead of multiplying it like the Master expected.

That's when the opportunity to write this book came along, dropped in my lap like a divine summons, along with my talented co-author and friend

Christy Stewart. In full disclosure, we are not single parents. We both have wonderful supportive husbands and five beautiful children between us.

We would not have chosen this project for ourselves. But God, who gives us better than we could dream, gave us the privilege of being the story tellers for single parents who have turned their own personal tragedies into triumph.

Our prayer is that all who read these stories will be inspired and encouraged as we bear witness to the healing, the joy, the blessing, and the beauty that comes from sacrifice for another and persevering through trials.

CHRISTY'S STORY

I have a secret, too. I never wanted to be a writer. Like my first child, this calling came to me as an unhappy surprise. I reacted like the child within my womb would two years later: face down on the floor kicking and screaming at the realization that *I* was not the one in control.

Nicknamed "the virgin Mary" by my collegiate classmates who misunderstood my quest for holiness, I stared in shock at the bright red lines that ran dark as sin across my pregnancy test, proving once and for all that God's plans are not my plans and I was indeed pregnant. His timing for this unplanned pregnancy was like his timing for me to be a writer: it couldn't have been worse. I didn't have time. I wasn't prepared.

He didn't seem to notice. As a matter of fact, it was as if he saw those red lines the way he saw all of the lines I had drawn in my life, as a place to start, rather than a place to stop. I hate it when he does that.

And so my writing career tumbled forward like my son as he took his first steps—soft and clumsy at first, precious and awkward at the same time, until one day, it took off running.

I wouldn't trade it for the world, you know: being a mother or being a writer. Both have brought me inexplicable joy. Each word was written, birthed onto the pages of this book with the same kind of intensive labor we suffer to bring our children into this world. The beauty of what is created casts a spell over us which begins in our hearts and ends in our minds, causing temporary amnesia so that we will be either dumb enough or passionate enough to do it all over again. And so we do, again and again.

I have three beautiful children now, who like God, continue to cross every line I draw. I was also fortunate enough to have found the perfect man who stops by whenever the Air Force allows him to be in the same country as me and our three children. The rest of the time I dabble in the art of single parenting to my kids who are as funny as their father and as rebellious as their mother ever was, providing all the fodder I need for a successful writing career at home. For these reasons, I thank God and my family, who never let a line keep them from crossing into my heart, the way I pray this book crosses into yours.

INTRODUCTION
BY RHONDA THOMAS
FOUNDER, SINGLE PARENT SUPPORT NETWORK

"In the heart of every single parent and in the heart of every child lies a treasure of dreams, gifts and talents waiting to be discovered…" – Rhonda Thomas

This book was inspired by the need to spread the wonderful news that anyone, if they choose, can make it through the most difficult challenges in life. Our Creator made us that way.

Parents are entrusted with one of the greatest and most difficult responsibilities ever given to mankind—raising and leading children. The most efficient way to fulfill this critical task is with two parents. The challenge becomes even more difficult when one parent is absent, creating a missing link in the family structure, causing hardships that most could never comprehend and that affect the family for generations to come.

A single parent can be anyone raising children alone:
- A widow or widower
- A divorced parent
- A biological mom or dad who has never been married
- A foster or adoptive single parent
- A single grandparent or other family member
- A parent whose spouse is incarcerated
- A parent whose spouse is gone for an extended period of time (e.g. for military service)
- A parent whose spouse is ill
- A woman who was a victim of rape
- A single parent who has chosen artificial insemination

Single parents come in all shapes and sizes. Some choose this life, while for others, it chooses them. But all of them have this in common: their lives teach us how far one person's love can reach, like a mama bird spreading her wings.

This story of the mother eagle from author Donna Partow's book *Becoming a Vessel God Can Use* beautifully expresses this journey and responsibility of the single parent:

"When the mother eagle is expecting her young, she prepares a large nest high on the edge of a cliff. She fashions it out of giant branches and sharp thorns. She then fills it with layer upon layer of soft feathers.

"When the baby eagles arrive and start getting all comfy-cozy in the nest, do you know what the mother eagle does? Each day she removes a few more feathers until, finally, the nest becomes unbearable. She does this deliberately, knowing full well that unless she forces her little ones out of their comfort zone, they'll never take that leap of faith. They'll never know what it means to soar.

"Well, finally the little eagles can take it no longer. They climb to the edge of the nest and look down into the giant chasm below. Their hearts are gripped with fear, but what they've got is so bad, the unknown could hardly be worse. They mount their courage and take the leap of faith, realizing that their wings are completely untested. They have no skill, no experience, no backup plan. They have absolutely no cause for confidence.

"The baby eagle continues plummeting toward the earth, and just when it seems all hope is lost the mother eagle swoops underneath it and allows it to mount up on her wings. For the first time in its life she knows what it means to soar. From that moment on, there's no holding it back. It is free from fear. Confident."

The Single Parent Support Network was formed to provide single parents with a soft place to land through emotional support, education, coaching, and encouragement on their path to successfully raising their children.

Visit us at www.supportforsingleparents.org.

photo by Bryan Crump

1 STEFANNIE POWELL–
CHERISHED AND REDEEMED

Stefannie Powell and her four teenage daughters got tattoos together last Saturday. They will readily admit that their home is "barely organized chaos," and uncontrollable laughter is so frequent that they have made a rule that if you can't make it to the bathroom to pee, at least get to the tile.

But amid the unconventional parenting, infectious giggles, shrills of laughter, talking over one another, and generally basking in the pleasure of their own company, they tell a story of joy that came from great sorrow. And they give God all the credit.

"God took these five broken, smashed-up girls and made us a family," says Stefannie. "There is no way I would have thought I would have recovered this much, added to my family, or have a job like this. I couldn't have fathomed it."

Four years ago, Stefannie's world changed in an instant when her husband of seventeen years blindsided her with a divorce. "It was excruciating. There are no words to describe the suffering. You only know it if you go through it, but you wouldn't ever wish it for anyone. Someone who I had loved and given everything to for seventeen years was now attacking me."

"Divorce was nothing I ever prepared for. It was not an option in my heart." But soon, against her will, her marriage was reduced to a "math solution."

"It is so heartbreaking because that's my life. I was thirty-five. I'd been married seventeen years, half of my life, and it's an equation? [No-fault divorce laws] totally dehumanize it. The fact that I stayed home for twelve years and took care of our kids and our neighbor's kids didn't matter. There was a time when if you'd been married for seventeen years and your husband cheated on you and left you, you'd be getting seventy-five percent of his income for life."

Instead, she and her two teenage daughters, Amanda and Kathryn, sixteen and thirteen at the time, were forced to sell their home ("a two-story reminder of broken promises"), give up their dog (who wasn't allowed in their new apartment), and leave the private Christian school they had attended. Stefannie started working nights and weekends flipping burgers at a rodeo arena in addition to her full-time job at their church, but she still wasn't making enough to pay the bills.

Despite their desperate situation, she believed God gave her a promise, a promise she had tattooed on her shoulder: I Peter 5:8-11. The passage reminds her that "there is suffering everywhere, but he will restore me and put me on a firm foundation. The suffering will not last forever."

Stefannie says, "From the moment their dad left, God moved in [my life] in a way he had never been because I never needed him in that way before. I went to what I knew would work: the Scripture. I slept with my Bible on my pillow, and every night when I went to bed exhausted without an ounce left, I would read the Psalms out loud. After a while, I found myself reading with such strength and boldness that I didn't know I had. I've always prayed for my kids, but that was a different sort of prayer."

She believes God also put every bitter divorced woman in her church in her path as a warning against the dangers of unforgiveness. She prayed, "Dear God, I will do whatever you want me to do as long as I won't be that. I don't want to be that."

So Stefannie began to look for the positive in the situation, no matter how small. "I embraced the things I couldn't do as a married person. I went out and got a tattoo. I wanted a tattoo my whole life, and my husband wouldn't let me. We pierced our ears up and down, got purple hair. We sat down one day and had a long conversation about what's positive about this [divorce]. We can run around in our t-shirts and underwear. We can stay in bed until noon. We went on vacation. We had never been on a trip that didn't involve a funeral or a family reunion."

Things weren't all positive. "We couldn't pay the bills," remembers Stefannie. "The girls would ask, 'Did you pay the electric bill?' I'd say, 'No, I was hoping they would leave me alone for a few months.' But the most dramatic change they made was welcoming teenage twins into their home.

"Katie and Kimmie were spending a lot of time at our house, a day or a week or whatever. I knew something wasn't right in the home, but until [the kids] speak up, there's nothing you can do. Finally, I said one time to Kimmie, 'Take it for what it's worth, but if you ever need a place to stay that's safe, I'm here.'"

"Two months later, the girls started talking about what was going on at home, and DHS removed them. They took a short detour with another family member, but I finally got them. October 18th. I called my daughter Amanda, 'I need to tell you something. I'm going to have twins.'

"When you look at the big picture of divorce, healing, and restoration, at the very lowest point, at the most financially draining, when I couldn't keep the utilities on, the absolute lowest point, God brought me two more. DHS calls and says, 'Can you still take these two kids?' 'Yes.' There was never a pause. My mind was made up when I told that to Kimmie."

But the financial reality of having two more kids began to sink in.

"I sat there so many nights. Working a full-time job, working on the weekends flipping burgers, still can't keep utilities on, that feeling of . . . I don't want to say 'hopelessness' because I knew the firm foundation was coming. I just didn't know how long it would take," says Stefannie.

Stefannie tells of one night when she had been working nine straight days from 7:30 a.m. to noon at the church and then from 1:00 p.m. to 2:00 a.m. flipping burgers at the rodeo arena an hour's drive north. On the last night, "I cried all the way home. I was pushing the 'this is not fair' button. Tim chose to leave, and I'm getting home from the Lazy E at 3 a.m. I don't understand, Lord. I know the victory is there, but I don't get it. What have I done to deserve this?"

She came home to all four girls sleeping in one room. "They were hanging off the sides of the bed. Half were on the floor. We couldn't have posed the picture. There could have been ten kids there; there were arms and legs everywhere. I remember that moment as if it were two minutes ago. For the first time since my husband left, I felt family again. It was whole. Just an incredible sense of peace."

She laughs, "So I turned the light on and woke them all up. 'Y'all get up. I cried all the way home. I miss y'all. I want you to talk to me.'" For the next hour, they giggled and laughed so hard they couldn't talk, until one unnamed daughter finally wet all over herself (hence, the new rule). "At that moment, we began another phase," says Stefannie. "We turned a corner. All these fiery arrows were still coming at us, but we didn't care."

"We spent our nights laughing. Literally, our lease was not renewed because we laughed too much," says Stefannie. "I'm cool with that. We just had a lot of fun. We got Netflix and spent hours on YouTube. We played games together, being loud and laughing. Even though DHS and their dad were getting worse, it didn't matter. We were in our own little bubble, and we didn't feel like anything could get to us."

The girls giggle as they tell about mattress surfing down stairs, flying over couches during games of "Extreme Spoons" (like the card game Spoons except you hide the spoons all over the house), and their "pizza roll phase" ("One of the great things about not having a man in the house is I don't have to cook," says Stefannie).

Weeks after they were forced to leave their apartment, Stefannie got a call from the Oklahoma Baptist Children's Home about a job in one of their cottages for single moms. For over a year now, she has served as a "family advisor" living in one of the cottages with her girls while being responsible for up to four other single-parent families living in the cottage as well.

"It's an incredible family ministry," says Stefannie. "It's called the Children's Hope Ministry. Our goal is to minister to the children through their moms, to break the generational bondage. The girls love to play with the kids. They get to see the results of moms who have not made wise choices. They learn a lot about choices and life and boundaries and natural consequences (that is my favorite word). It's incredible. It's incredibly hard at times, too. From the single mom perspective, I've got my four kids, and then at any given time I've got from five to eleven other people in my cottage that I'm also responsible for."

"We've got moms in the program from nineteen to forty-four years of age. A single mom can find herself homeless in a snap. We give them a place to live. What we do is say, 'Now, without that to worry about, let's change your life. Let's make your generation of children different from yours.' We help them get their GED, finish school, get jobs, receive counseling, learn to cook and clean, understand basic finances, discipline children—whatever that individual mom needs."

"When you look at the pay, it's ridiculous. People at McDonald's make more than I do. But I don't pay for housing, I don't pay utilities, and I get food also. But who gets to be with their kids?" Stefannie marvels. "Single moms don't get to be stay-at-home moms. I worked at the church, and I loved it. But I wanted to be at home with my kids. I really feel strongly about that. The kids will grow up and go away. I only have them for a short amount of time. I have four chances to be a good mom. I have unlimited chances to do other stuff."

"One thing that I have found encouraging about being a single parent, for us, is we have found a great deal of freedom out of this horrible, horrible situation. If I were still married, I would not have Katie and Kimmie. When I got that phone call, my husband would have said 'no.' I would not have them if I were still married, and we would have missed this incredible blessing. Our friend that comes over most every Friday and Saturday night—that would not have happened. The kids that are over here all the time—those things never would have happened. The hours and hours of playing spades, or wrestling on the floor, or just talking—none of that would have happened."

"We're not a normal family," interjects Kathryn. "We love each other so much. We're so close, it's weird."

"So many times," says Stefannie. "I sit in awe of what God has done in my kids' lives, the healing that He's brought, the hope that they have now that they didn't have before. It's incredible."

On a recent Saturday, all five girls went together to Kansas to get tattoos. Their selections reveal just how deep the healing goes.

Amanda, who began drawing for the first time after the divorce, chose one of her own creations—a heart tied up with rope.

Kathryn chose an infinity symbol with Isaiah 48:13 in the middle and the words, "I am His, and He is mine." She says of her selection, "Since my dad left, and I could never count on him, I would always struggle with [the idea that] I'm never going to mean anything to any guy. God just really showed me, 'Kathryn, you're always mine, and you are always going to be in my hands.' That's the verse he showed me. It talks about how once God's done something, you can't undo it."

And the tiny 4'11" blond twins who have been through unspeakable horrors and been thrown away by their family?

Kimmie had "Cherished" tattooed on her wrist.

Katie had "Redeemed" tattooed on her back.

Kimmie softly adds, "There's a verse that we've talked about before, Genesis 50:20, about the story of Joseph. He says, 'You meant to harm me, but God used it for the saving of many lives.' God saved all of us through the divorce. It hurt everyone, of course. But He brought it back together."

photos by Amanda Powell

2 MOYA AND STELLA SMITH –

A DAUGHTER'S ADMIRATION:
THE GREATEST REWARD OF GOOD PARENTING

Few women ever rise to the rank of colonel in the Air Force, and fewer still come from the humble beginnings of Stella Smith. Col. Smith has traveled the world, has met heads of state, has dined in palaces, and is currently responsible for more than fifteen hundred airmen and twenty-seven airplanes. But of all the leaders she's met, it's her mother who earns her greatest respect and admiration.

Stella's father abandoned her and her mother Moya when Stella was only a few months old.

When her husband left, British-native Moya had only been in America for less than a year, didn't know how to drive, and had never even handled a dollar bill. "He met her, married her, and brought her over here, and then left her," says Stella. He left her with a four-month-old baby, the rent paid up, and the promise of $100 a month in child support (which rarely materialized). His sister even came to take the family crib away. Moya's plight was so desperate that her attorney's secretary took her in for several weeks until she could get a waitressing job.

8

Throughout Stella's childhood they constantly struggled financially. Both admit they were "literally close to starving at times." Stella says, "I still can't look at a bologna sandwich without being sad" because of all the "yucky" free school lunches she felt obliged to eat—often the only food she had.

Stella's mother Moya doesn't believe she did anything extraordinary in raising her exceptional daughter. She says with typical British understatement (and charming British accent), "I was just there for her. You just do what you think is right."

But Stella's mother passed on to her young daughter more than she knew. "She was a really good mom, a phenomenal mom," says Stella. "The things she taught me influence everything about me."

"The biggest thing she taught me is to look for opportunities. She never let our station in life limit my ability to dream big—ever. When I look at what the Air Force offers its people, it's similar to the way my mom made me look at the world. It doesn't matter what you started with or where you came from. It equalizes everyone. If you have a good attitude and look for opportunities, you can do anything."

Col. Smith's long list of accomplishments certainly attests to the truth of that belief. A graduate of the Air Force Academy and the Air War College, she has served for almost twenty-four years in the Air Force on eleven different bases, in Iraq, and on Capitol Hill. As legislative liaison for the Air Force, she visited forty-seven countries in thirty-six months, accompanying Members of Congress and facilitating meetings with heads of state.

But she is quick to downplay her own career and sing the praises of the single mother who raised her to expect greatness. Stella recalls that although they had no money for extras, her mother used all the resources they did have to find opportunities for her daughter, including free dance lessons, free trumpet lessons, and free summer camps. "It didn't matter what we didn't have; she was going to go find what she could for me."

Stella tells story after story of her mother's sacrifice, perseverance, and determination to give her daughter the best life she could despite the cards life had handed them.

"My mom has had so many unfair things happen in her life," says Stella.

"She came to expect it. She wouldn't stand up for herself, but she would stand up for me. My mom is a real introvert. She's not going to talk about herself or brag about herself, but she is a very smart, educated lady. And she took all those skills and talents and focused them on what she could do for me."

"Even though she was such an introvert, when it mattered to me, she came out of her shell and went to town. Like when my high school was calculating the class rankings in a very unfair way, counting all the classes equally. My mom marched her happy butt right down there into the guidance counselor's office and got it changed. She was not going to have me not go to the Air Force Academy because another girl got a higher grade in art history than I got in AP chemistry. She was not seeking an unfair advantage, she just wanted a fair shake for me. And of course, it helped so many other people because I was not the only one in that situation."

Moya also passed on her work ethic. "We were basically destitute at times and dependent on government assistance, but even then, my mom wanted to work so badly to support me, she would go to get a day job. Whatever was available—bottling 7-Up, putting handles on knives, driving a taxi for railroad workers. She wanted to teach me that you work no matter what. And the way the system was set up then, you actually lost more money than you made [because the income was taxed and government benefits were not]. She once came home from work with her arm in a sling because she got her hand caught in the machine at the knife factory. It was incredibly scary because she was everything to me."

Moya's sacrifices included taking out a loan just to pay her daughter's initial uniform deposit, and taking time off work and traveling to another city so Stella could get the required Air Force physical exam. But the one thing that Stella most admired her mother for was the courage she showed in putting her only daughter on the plane to the Air Force Academy.

"I always knew that I was going to go to college after high school. First, that was a bold dream for her to give me, but I didn't have a concept of how much it cost. I didn't know my friends' parents were saving. I just knew my mom was going to make happen somehow." Fortunately, Stella did well enough in school to be accepted into the Air Force Academy, which is free, but she still realizes the self-sacrifice her mother made in putting her on that plane.

"I'm an only child, and she's sending me who knows where. Living in Buffalo, New York, we had never been anywhere west of Michigan. I cried all the way to Newark. When I got to Denver, I called her (this is before cell phones) and said, 'Mom, everybody else on this flight has a ticket through to Colorado Springs. I'm not sure what to do. Wait, I see a guy in a uniform. I'll ask him.' Click. This is the last call she gets from her seventeen-year-old. Two weeks later she gets a letter from me. You can't call. When you get to the Academy, they just start yelling at you. You're in basic training. I really admire her for helping me pursue my dreams."

Moya consistently supported Stella encouraging her to continue at the Academy and when she considered quitting her Air Force career.

Stella remembers calling home and saying, "I can't do this, I need to come home."

But Moya never said okay. She also never said no.

"Do you have a test coming up?" she would ask.

"Yes, I have a test tomorrow."

"Have you studied?" Moya would press.

"Yes."

"Do you need to study some more?"

"Yes."

"Well, go study for your test. I can't get you a ticket tonight because AAA is closed. But call me tomorrow," she would say knowing the next day the test would be fine.

"How perfect is that?" raves Stella. "I will never forget it. She has always been so supportive, even when it was to her own cost in a way, because she knew that keeping me in the Air Force life would mean that she was going to be alone."

In spite of all that Moya suffered, she never spoke poorly of Stella's father to her. "I really admire her for that," says Stella. "I knew when the checks weren't coming because we ate beans on toast or I couldn't get new shoes for school, but she never said anything. When I asked if I could see my father, she would say, 'When you get older, you can go see him. But I don't want to see him.' Not in a mean way though. I think that was a really good way to handle it."

Stella did eventually meet her father at age twenty when she traveled to Kentucky to see her paternal grandmother. "I had told myself that he hadn't seen me all these years because he didn't know where I was. That made it easier for me. Then I realized he lived next door to my grandmother, who had been calling me and sending me gifts all these years, so that burst my bubble. He knew where I was. His teenagers [from another marriage] both had cars, and I didn't have food?"

Their meeting was brief. He said, "I guess your mother told you it was all my fault. I figured that would be easier for you."

Stella replied, "No. She taught me to think for myself."

And she left—leaving behind any illusions of who her father might be but only cementing her conviction of the woman her mother was.

These days, although they live thousands of miles apart, the mutual admiration between mother and daughter is as strong as ever. Moya says, "Stella doesn't realize how talented she is in many ways. When she compares herself to her peers, she thinks she's normal, but at the Academy, all those kids were state superstars. Even now, she doesn't seem to realize that she's doing something extraordinary."

That's something else they have in common.

3 DR. YVONNE PENNINGTON— MOVING MOUNTAINS

"Move that Bus!" shouts Ty Pennington, now famous for this familiar phrase on ABC's hit TV show *Extreme Home Makeover*. But long before he was moving buses, his mom, Dr. Yvonne Pennington, was moving mountains to get him there.

Excitement, passion, and non-stop energy float to the top of Ty's hyper TV personality, making him perfect for his job. These qualities are the silver linings of his lifelong battle with Attention Deficit Hyperactivity Disorder [ADHD]. But few people know the difficulties the Pennington family faced before Ty became a household name.

Yvonne remembers as a child, in the days before doctors considered ADHD a disorder, she "never got in trouble, and [my brother] Donnie got in trouble for everything. He started running away when he was twelve. My father had beaten him with a belt. The next morning his [window] screen was gone. A year later my father hired a private detective and found him working on a ranch in Texas. Now I know it was ADHD. He was so impulsive. They didn't tell me what he was doing wrong. The first time [he ran away] he hitchhiked to Texas; the second time he went to Illinois where our older brother was."

Yvonne's love for Donnie matched her hatred for the way ADHD children like her brother were being treated and would eventually motivate her to change not just Ty's world, but the rest of ours, too.

Years later, as a young college girl who moved back home after losing her college scholarship because she couldn't afford textbooks, Yvonne met a talented musician (and the future father of her children) who was just beginning to make a name for himself. "Gary and I were talking on the phone every night, and finally we just decided that we would get married."

With the same impulsiveness her son Ty is known for, she left. "I had to get to Gary, and I didn't have a car. But I had a really large straw purse. I crammed all my clothes in there. I convinced my father to drive me over to the bus station to say good-bye to my [college] friends one last time. By the time they heard from me next, I was married. I was twenty-one. I mean, I should have known better!"

Shortly after giving birth to their first child, Wynn, Yvonne started to realize Gary had a drinking problem. "My parents were teetotalers, so I didn't know what normal drinking was. He would work as a musician and run up a tab, and by the end of the night he had drunk up all the money he had made. Eventually, he became a carpenter's helper, too, so he was making a little bit he couldn't drink up."

The night she went into labor with Wynn, she and Gary drove to the nearest charity hospital. "I had been squirreling back twenty-five whole dollars of the grocery money. So on the way, I took out the money I had squirreled away and handed it to Gary. I told him, 'Okay, I want you to go and buy as many diapers and bottles as you can with this money.' He dropped me off at the hospital and came back a few hours later with a case of beer and a box of cigars. No bottles, no diapers, and I was to go home the next day."

"This is hard to talk about, even years later," she says as tears stream down, gently crossing the soft lines that once framed her smile. As a clinical psychologist, Dr. Pennington is not used to talking. "Usually my patients do all the talking, and I do all the listening."

Yvonne tried for many years to make her marriage work, but shortly after giving birth to Ty, Gary's behavior became increasingly dangerous for her and their boys. One day while at work, her neighbor called frantically. "There is smoke coming out the bottom of your door, and the kids are inside! The babysitter is in there. I can't get her awake." Yvonne rushed home to find the babysitter, "drunk-as-a-skunk," passed out while the dinner burned on the stove. The babysitter had told Gary when she arrived that she was drunk and couldn't work, but he left them anyway. Ty was a year old, and Wynn was two. "It burned the pans up, and it was pretty much about to catch the whole place on fire. But we got them out, and I fired her."

The last straw fell when Gary stole the rent money, purchased a gun, and pointed it at her. "I thought, I need to get out of here," says Yvonne. Every night for two weeks, Gary would wait in the parking lot of their apartment building. "When I would get home, I would run for it and try to get in the front door without him killing me. That's how I became a single parent." Ty was two, and Wynn was three.

Yvonne went back to school, graduated, and got a job as a teacher in the same elementary school where her boys went. "I worked as an English teacher for awhile. Eventually I became interested in the field of psychology. I wanted to get into it." One of her first case studies was Ty.

"Second grade was when Ty was diagnosed [with ADHD]. He was spending every day in the principal's office. I was working on my Masters, and I asked the principal if I could do another case study, but this time I wanted to observe the worst kid in school. She said, 'Yvonne, you know who that is, don't you?'"

"There was a new behavior disorder teacher that year, and I asked her if she would go in and write down what [Ty] was doing for thirty minutes. It was unbelievable. He was wearing his desk! He'd put this piece over one shoulder and would run around the room... in second grade! You know, I had gotten so used to it, to where I didn't see it. If I could just keep him from darting out in front of cars and stuff, I was happy."

To say Ty was energetic is an understatement. "I mean, he did jump off of the roof twice! I was in the kitchen and out of the corner of my eye saw something cutting through the blinds. I ran outside, and sure enough, there he was in the shrubbery. He [had] climbed up the drain spout and thought, 'This will get a laugh!' and jumped. Oh, I didn't laugh. I said, 'Dad gone, Ty! Don't you have any good sense?!' But I didn't punish him. What good would it do? He was impulsive. He was the typical ADHD child. It ran in the family."

Ty's high energy and willingness to push the boundaries is what helped launch him to success on *Extreme Home Makeover*. But as a child, it wasn't so great. "He would have stomachaches in the morning because school was just so painful. He knew he would be in the principal's office. I just said, 'I know it's hard, sweetie; but I'm working on a way.'"

The token economy became the way Yvonne helped Ty exercise control over his impulsive urges. "I learned about it in a course. I tried it, and it worked. I had to figure out what the payoff would be. I had a teacher go in [his classroom] and watch him for two hours and tell me how long his attention span was. She came out and said, 'Ten seconds.'" Yvonne asked another teacher to spend a month in his classroom. She bought a bunch of coasters from a going-out-of-business sale and for every ten seconds he was paying attention, he got a token. It turned his life around. "Pretty soon he was up to twenty seconds, thirty seconds, and after a month we were up to a half hour."

Originally, Ty earned extra recess in exchange for tokens, but later his mom discovered that his favorite thing was the craft box. "I would supervise him for a half an hour working in the craft box, and he loved it! Remember those pot holders you can make with the loops? I put those in there. He loved making those. I still have one of the potholders he made. Eventually I introduced him to a hammer and a saw and nails, supervising him. He started at the age of seven. By the time he was nine, he made a three-story tree house! All he had was the hammer, a saw, and nails. He found lumber from the side of the road. He hired the neighborhood kids and paid them in comic books! He was so proud of himself!"

Yvonne worked hard "to find something that he could be good at. So I paid for private art lessons for Ty. I scrimped and saved. He really needed that for his self esteem. My parents had done the same stretching for me."

From musician to model to carpenter on TLC's *Trading Spaces* to host of

Extreme Home Makeover, Ty Pennington seemed destined for fame. But Yvonne says, "I never expected he would be doing this. I mean, gosh, through his twenties Ty had a really tough time. He was always losing his keys in the car, and he'd lose his wallet. In the prefrontal lobes, you don't mature as quickly when you're ADHD."

It was during those times that she slowly and intentional pulled back her support so that Ty could learn to stand on his own two feet. After losing his job due to a motorcycle accident, Ty was struggling to make ends meet. "Ty was unable to model after the accident and lost his art job because he forgot to call his boss when he needed to miss work for his physical therapy appointments." It was at this critical moment when, Yvonne remembers, "I went over to see him. It was the dead of winter, and the lights had been turned off. The water had been turned off. The heat had been turned off. And he's sitting there in the dark. I brought him dinner, and I left him. I said, 'I'm sure you'll figure this out, sweetie.' I didn't give him any money because I didn't want him to think that I would rescue him. That was about the hardest thing I ever did."

Eventually, Yvonne's little boy grew up and matured into the guy we know now, one of *People* magazine's *Sexiest Men Alive*. After being spotted doing carpentry by a TLC network producer, who said, "He is hot!," Ty was cast for his first TV series, *Trading Spaces*. Even though Ty is a celebrity, Yvonne says, "He's still the same. He's such a sweetheart. He really is."

She's not the only one who thinks so. "Women have always been throwing themselves at Ty. He had a girlfriend for twelve years, but he works eighteen hours a day, seven days a week, making a relationship hard to sustain. He would come home, do laundry, and then get on a plane and be gone again."

Though he is hard to catch, Ty Pennington can be found Sunday nights as the host of HLN's show, *American Journey*. He attributes his televisions hosting skills to his mom, telling her, "When I sit down and get these people to tell their stories, that is you coming through me."

Yvonne encourages other parents of children with ADHD that no matter how bad it gets, "to notice what they do right, because most of the time all they hear is what they do wrong. Ty eventually learned not to dart into traffic or jump off roofs!"

And because of her, Ty Pennington is stopping traffic and building roofs everywhere he goes.

4 ANGELA SHEPHARD –THE FIGHTER

Angela Shephard is a fighter. She has the tenacity of a bulldog. Nothing and no one will stop her when she sets her mind to something, especially when it comes to taking care of her two sons.

"If I start something, I want to finish it, no matter how long it takes," she says referring to the ten years it took to graduate from college.

She fought for her marriage. She and her husband—high school sweethearts—stayed together for twelve years. From the outside they seemed to have the perfect marriage, until the post-traumatic stress following his service in Iraq and subsequent physical abuse left her no option other than calling 911.

She fought for her youngest son Kendrick. When a pediatrician discounted her concerns about his development, she pressed until a neurologist discovered her baby had suffered a stroke shortly after birth. Then she prayed for his healing like only a mother can. And God answered her prayers like only He can. Kendrick's miraculous recovery amazed his mother and his occupational therapist when they saw the little boy who was unable to stand only weeks before running up and down the hall on her next visit.

She fought for her eldest son Leo. When he struggled in school, Angela advocated tirelessly for the flexibility and specialized instruction he needed to succeed. Failure was not an option. "I could not put my son in [those] schools," she states flatly of their public school district. "I would be setting him up for failure because he has ADD [Attention Deficit Disorder]. He needs special attention."

She got a diagnosis. She moved her family to a more cooperative school district. She met with the principal and teachers. They set up a plan. She joined a support group CHADD (Children & Adults with Attention-Deficit/Hyperactivity Disorder). She set up her own non-profit organization for kids with disabilities.

When asked how a single parent could find the time and energy to do these things, Angela simply says, "I had to. I had to put one foot in front of the other and do what was necessary for my son. If anybody has to go through what I did to get help for my son, I want to save them some of those steps. It was really hard."

Even when she was laid off after the economic collapse in 2008 and lost her home, she refused to be a victim. She was unemployed for six months before she finally found a job at the Feed the Children call center. When income from that job still didn't cover the rent, utilities, and grocery bills for herself and two teenage boys, she got an entry-level job in medical billing so she could learn the business. She eventually hopes to get her own medical billing clients and work for herself from home so she can spend more time with her boys.

She wears a gold ring with a cross made of small diamonds on her left hand. "When I look at this, I know I'm not alone," she explains. "God is my husband. I may not have a husband now, but He is my provider. And whenever I feel like I just don't know where the money is going to come from, when I'm about to have a nervous breakdown, I know that He is going to intervene. It always happens."

One tangible way she believes God provided was being selected as one of the forty single mothers with two boys to receive a $2,000 empowerment grant from NBA star Kevin Durant through the Single Parent Support Network. "I don't know how others used theirs, but I used mine to pay bills," she says.

She and her sons, now ages thirteen and fifteen, still struggle every day to make ends meet. The hardest struggle, however, is seeing her sons' heartbreak.

"I don't feel like Dad loves us like he used to anymore," her youngest son Kendrick recently confided to her.

"Why do you say that?" she probed.

"Because he always says, 'You call me if you ever need anything,' but when I call, he never answers his phone," he responded.

He then shared how his dad had promised to buy him an iPod for Christmas, but then when he saw his stepbrother's new iPod and asked when he would be getting his, his dad said, "I don't know if I'll be getting you one."

With her typical dogged determination, Angela did her best to heal her son's wound.

"My kids understand that gifts are not everything. My kids have never really asked for expensive things, but I scraped together money and went down to the pawn shop and got him an iPod for Christmas. I put a cover on it so he couldn't tell it was used."

Single parenting has revealed Angela's inner strength and deepened her faith. "I got to see how strong I really was. I never thought I could work sixty hours a week, but you do what you got to do. Until you actually hit rock bottom and rely totally on God, you don't see Him in everything. I see Him in even trivial things now."

"God has control over everything that happens in the world. That's how I see my life. God has the ability to come in and make all this trouble and sorrow go away. But He hasn't. Not because he doesn't love me. It's because it's something that I need to learn from—to move to the next level in my life."

From the time of our interview to the publishing of this book, God has answered Angela's prayers once again with a pay raise and promotion at work. But more importantly for her, the promotion means she no longer has to work the night shift as she has for the past three years, so she can spend more time with her boys.

5 CHRISTY JOHNSON–
THE POWER OF FORGIVENESS

A single mom who attended one of Christy Johnson's classes on forgiveness shared her first impression: "First, she looks like Barbie. She's tall and blonde and beautiful, and she looks like she has her stuff together. I'm sitting in my chair thinking, 'What can this woman teach me? She has the perfect life.' Then she starts telling her story, and everybody's mouth just dropped. She said, 'Let me tell you about forgiveness. My son should be fifteen, but he's not. My son was killed in a car accident, and my ex-husband is to blame. He was high on five different drugs, and that's what killed my son.'"

A self-proclaimed "relationship junkie," Christy reveals with breathtaking honesty what she has learned through heartache and tragedy about healthy relationships and forgiveness. Her words of wisdom are hard-won from a lifetime of seeking validation from men, her ten-year marriage to an abusive drug addict, and finally the death of her two-year-old son Jake in a tragic car accident.

Christy shares her humor, insights, and shocking vulnerability about her failures in speaking engagements across the country and in her upcoming book, *Rehab for Love Junkies: Seven Must-Haves for Soul-Healthy Relationships.* Even more than the helpful checklists in her book, though, her own real-life example of forgiving the unforgivable is her most powerful tool for giving hope to others.

"I look at everything as sifted through the hand of God," she says. "If he allows something to happen in your life, he is going to give you the grace to endure it. So to be mad at your ex-husband, why not be mad at God because it first must be sifted through his hand? Unforgiveness does nothing but damage us."

Christy believes God taught her forgiveness through those ten tumultuous years of marriage, "The only way we can learn forgiveness is to suffer an offense. In a marriage, that's where people can hurt us the most. If I don't learn to forgive, God gives me another chance—a re-take, another opportunity to surrender and forgive. I would pray, 'God, can't you change him? Can't you see what he's doing?' Nothing changed. God gave me opportunity after opportunity after opportunity to learn how to forgive."

"You have to practice. It's like a muscle. Like faith. If you can't forgive a small offense, you won't be able to forgive a big offense. Daily surrender those things. It becomes a habit and a lifestyle."

She points to the biblical story of Joseph who was sold into slavery by his brothers and wrongfully imprisoned by Egyptians but who saved both Egypt and Israel from starvation. "God was teaching him how to forgive, so he could save the world," she says. "God allowed him to go through all this adversity to teach him to forgive."

So about the accident her husband caused, she says simply, "I forgave him. The power of God was so strong. I knew if I didn't forgive, I'd go straight back to bondage. The Lord has really given me a genuine compassion to see him healed and restored."

Christy emphasizes the awful weight of bitterness on the offended party, "Bitterness is a poison. [Forgiving someone] doesn't mean they are excused from the consequences of what they did. It doesn't mean what they did was right. It doesn't release the offender, but it releases us."

Christy's greatest liberation, however, came when she experienced forgiveness herself. Throughout her life and even during her marriage, Christy continually anesthetized her pain through relationships with men. After taking out a victim's protection order against her husband, she was sitting home alone one weekend. "I don't know how to be alone. I said, 'God, why am I like this?' He revealed to me, 'Christy, the reason you have always needed a relationship [with a man] is because you didn't have my identity. You sought approval, affirmation, identity, and affection from men because you didn't know how to get it from me; and one man was never enough, so you had to have other men."

"God revealed to me in that moment that there was nothing I could do that would make him love me any less. No matter how badly I failed, he wouldn't reject me. And no matter how wonderful something was that I did, it wasn't going to make him love me anymore. I was free to be me for the first time in my life. From that moment on, it was like this huge identity revelation that completely empowered me. It was liberating. It was the most liberating feeling I've ever had in my life. I finally could just be me."

Christy is now sharing her new freedom and liberating joy with the world as a talented and entertaining Christian writer and speaker. In the following two essays, she recounts the story of her son Jake's death and her son Garrett's recovery and reveals her struggles as a parent to her daughter Brittany.

An Escort to Heaven

By Christy Johnson

The doctor's words ricocheted through my mind. *Unfortunately, Jake didn't make it.* I slammed the phone on the receiver in disbelief. Sobbing, I collapsed on the counter.

My fiancé grabbed my purse and rushed me to his truck. By the time we got to the hospital, the sight of my five-year-old son, Garrett, was a shock. The blood from the wounds on his face had already turned a crusty black. At first glance, it looked like all of his teeth had been knocked out from the impact.

"Hi Garrett," I said as I forced a smile and leaned down to kiss his forehead. "Where did you get this stuffed bear? He sure is cute."

"From the ambulance man," Garrett said with gleaming eyes.

Like most young boys, Garrett was fascinated by emergency professionals. His favorite TV program was *Rescue 911*. Before the show would start, he lined up all of his electronic emergency vehicles on the carpet in front of the TV. His collection of fire trucks, police cars, and ambulances were ready for action. I never imagined he would be a victim in his own episode.

Suddenly the curtains swung open, and the doctor entered the room. "We need to check for internal injuries. Since Garrett can't swallow the contrast dye, we'll need to insert a tube up his nose and down his throat to inject the dye for the x-ray. Would you like to stay in the room and hold his hand?"

"Of course," I gulped, fighting back tears. Never mind that I couldn't even watch my own blood being drawn.

The rest of the day was a blur. Between all the phone calls and the multitude of visitors I barely remember a thing, except that an odd but welcome sense of peace began to settle on me. Later that day, the doctor gave the first bit of good news.

"Garrett has a hairline fracture to his jaw but the x-rays show no internal injuries."

The swelling in Garrett's face prevented expression, but I could tell he was trying to smile. He didn't want me to worry. Soon, he drifted off to sleep.

The next morning, I dropped little squirts of juice into Garrett's mouth with a baby eyedropper. "What's wrong, Mommy?"

"Nothing," I lied. Despite the peace I felt, the truth was I didn't have a clue how I was going to tell him about his two-year-old little brother, Jake.

"Why don't you wait until Garrett asks about Jake?" my friends advised. Initially, that sounded like a good plan, but four days later he still hadn't asked.

With the funeral fast approaching, my fiancé was concerned. "Do you want me to talk to him?" John asked.

"No," I sighed. "I have to do this myself."

Garrett's face brightened as I entered his room. "Look, Mommy! Bruce brought me some more stuffed animals. *And* the Transformer I wanted—Optimus Prime."

"That's nice, Honey." I scooted a chair beside his bed.

"Garrett," I began.

"Yeah, Mommy?"

My body felt suddenly paralyzed.

"What would you say if I told you…" I stalled, gasping for air. "It's Jake. Jake didn't make it." Tears streamed down my face. I couldn't even look up.

"Mom, I already know."

You already know? My jaw fell to my chest. "What do you mean, 'You already know?'"

"After the accident, I got to go to heaven with Jake." Garrett swooped Optimus Prime into the air. He made gun sounds as he beat up his invisible enemies, "Jake got to go in, but God told me it wasn't my time."

Suddenly I was on the edge of my seat. "What was heaven like?"

"Mommy!" Garrett's eyes squinted with apparent irritation. He set his Transformer down. A bewildered look spread across his face. "Mommy! I can't tell you that!"

"Why not?" I insisted.

"It's a surprise!"

"I'm sure God won't mind if you tell me, Garrett. He'll understand—I'm your *mother*."

"No, Mommy, I *can't!*"

"Why not?"

"Cuz. God told me it's a secret."

He went back to playing with his toys while I sat back in my chair flabbergasted. *Garrett sure picked a good time to start keeping secrets.* In the past he flunked confidentiality, but now his lips were locked.

The peace that Garrett felt magnified my own. We both spoke at Jake's funeral. I held the microphone while he shared his story about escorting his little brother to heaven in front of hundreds of attendees. In the days and weeks following his release from the hospital, I tried to squeeze details out of Garrett, but he never uttered another clue. His childlike trust amazed me, yet I fought skepticism. Did Garrett really take a trip to heaven or was his story a figment of his five-year-old imagination?

Preschoolers can make up some enchanting stories. If it was make-believe, however, it worked for him. He didn't grieve like the grief recovery books that well-meaning friends had given me predicted. He never had a nightmare about the accident. And even though his biological father received a deferred sentence for negligent homicide for driving under the influence of several narcotics, Garrett held no bitterness toward his dad. Even so, I pried and pried to get him to open up about his trip to heaven.

Until I found the reason for his peculiar silence.

One day, I was reading my morning devotional and came across a story in the Bible about a man who had been to heaven. He couldn't describe what he saw because it was a secret. I was spellbound. In the book of II Corinthians, the apostle Paul says that he was caught up in the "third heaven" where he heard inexpressible things—*things that man was not permitted to tell.*

Paul experienced the same kind of secret quest that Garrett had witnessed.

I lingered over the verses for a moment. *What Garrett saw, he wasn't permitted to tell. That's why Garrett couldn't disclose details about his heavenly encounter. It really was a secret. It wasn't a fairy tale…it was a faith tale.*

I closed my Bible. As the pages fluttered together, my doubts finally vanished. Who was I to contend with a divine mystery? Awestruck, I realized that his journey to heaven empowered him with peace in the midst of disaster. Never again will I doubt the faith of a child, nor God's ability to provide peace in the midst of tragedy.

Especially to his precious little children.

Jake's death changed my destiny. I started writing because of the peace and joy I experienced in the midst of sorrow. In a way, you could say Jake's legacy lives on in me. As for Garrett, today he is twenty. Although he still speaks little of his trip to heaven, his countenance of peace has never left. I know God has a strong purpose for the secret he entrusted with Garrett that day. As much as I long to understand more, one thing I know for sure—heaven is flowing with peace and joy, because Garrett came back with a lifetime supply.

"Down to the Top"

By Christy Johnson

When my first marriage ended in divorce, I thought the shame of dealing with drug addiction was a thing of the past. I never dreamed it would come back to haunt me.

My daughter Brittany was always so quiet and responsible, but after she graduated from high school things changed. My timid freckle-faced artist morphed into a loud and obnoxious druggie. Of all people, she should know better—the first ten years of her life were filled with chaos due to her father's drug habit. Even so, I couldn't help but blame myself.

I hated it when my friends asked how Brittany was doing. Their daughters were going to college and getting married. What was I supposed to say— she's smoking crack and popping pills? Internal critiques harassed me daily but like a belt that was one notch too tight, I stuffed the shame.

I wanted her to continue living at home after graduation so she could attend a local college, but Brit couldn't wait to move out. She thought I had too many rules. Her only trips home were to catch up on laundry. When I asked about her classes, she got defensive. Then during her second semester she announced, "I'm not going back. I'm flunking most of my classes anyway."

I had suspicions earlier, but now it was hard to deny. Her constricted pupils and personality changes were all too familiar. I offered counseling for her, but she refused and met every confrontation with bitter scorn—until the phone call I got after she was picked up for drug possession.

"Mom, I'm in jail. Can you bail me out?"

Her request was as casual as if she were asking to borrow a pair of jeans. She seemed to delight in the shock value of her behavior.

How could she make choices like this? Especially after what drugs have done to our family?

By the time bail was arranged, Brittany was transferred to the county jail. When I arrived the next morning, she skipped to the car like I was picking her up from kindergarten. "Jail wasn't so bad," she boasted. "I even made some friends."

I fumed inside. I shouldn't have bailed her out! She needs to learn a lesson.

"Oh, and guess who transported me last night from the Warr Acres jail to county?"

I shrugged.

"Pastor Michael."

"Really?"

Officer Anderson was on staff at our church for years. Of course, we still referred to him as Pastor Michael even though he now served on the Warr Acres police force.

"Yeah, I got the mini sermon-slash-lecture on the way, but hey, what else could I expect?"

I mused at the Lord's providence. Of all the officers in the city, she received a divine escort. Brittany may have been the only person in Pastor Michael's "mobile congregation" that day, but he delivered a sermon just the same.

"Brittany, don't you know there's nowhere you can go that God can't find you?"

She rolled her eyes.

Brittany's freedom came with a huge price after her drug bust: court costs, attorney fees, and drug tests. I hated to see her endure so much, but I prayed that she would learn from her mistakes and want to come back home. One fall day while cooking dinner, I got a call from an unfamiliar number. "Hi Mom, it's Brit. Just wanted to let you know where I'm staying. I met a great new friend. Her name is Brittany, too."

Her friend still lived at home with her parents. Tears smudged my recipe. Why would she prefer to live with another family rather than her own? I didn't even feel like cooking. It wasn't the same without Brittany at home.

For several months, Brittany remained unemployed and stayed with her friend. I pleaded with the Lord. Please don't let them continue to enable her. Then, just before the spring semester of college, her friend's mother laid down the law. She worked for an attorney and required her own children, as well as Brittany, to sign a "Family Life Contract." The contract listed behavior required in exchange for free room and board. One requirement was full-time college attendance.

When Brittany told me about the contract, I couldn't help but laugh inside. She collided right back into the very thing she was running from—rules. Along with these new boundaries, however, her friend's mother also exercised compassion. She convinced the attorney she worked for to represent Brittany pro-bono on her drug charges.

Now that constant expectations weren't coming from me, gradually our relationship began to improve. As much as I prayed for Brittany, it seems God was more concerned about working patience and forgiveness in me. We still don't see eye-to-eye on everything, but at least now we're able to enjoy each other's company again. On Saturday mornings we grab a cup of coffee and hunt down vintage items at local estate sales. Most of all, I enjoy her pesky sense of humor. No one can make me laugh like Brittany.

Her life still has ups and downs. After a recent DUI, I fell on my knees again and sobbed. She knows better. How can she be so rebellious?

I felt the Lord speak to my spirit. "If Brittany walked in obedience, would you take the credit?"

"Well, yes," I stammered. "I raised her in church."

"Then you would be full of pride."

"What do you mean?"

"You would be taking credit for your daughter's decisions. She has her own free will to make choices. I was the perfect parent and my children rebelled. That doesn't make me any less righteous."

I had to admit. I had never thought about that before. "The best thing you can do for Brittany is to walk in forgiveness and be there for her when she is ready—ready to listen."

A recess bell rang from the school down the street and startled me. I'm sure I'd heard it a hundred times before but for some reason, it was louder today. Maybe that's how Brittany will be. Someday, she'll hear the message loud and clear. I just have to wait until she's ready.

I've since learned the best way to influence my daughter is to let my own life speak. Today when my friends ask how Brittany is doing I no longer lower my head in shame. My children are not a badge of honor. They are human too, and like some of us, sometimes they have to hit bottom before they're willing to look up. So I've come up with a catch phrase to speak the truth in faith. Now when my friends ask how Brittany is doing, I simply say, "She's on her way down to the top."

Yes…the top—that's her destiny.

6 MIKE METCALF–
"JUST A PROUD DAD"

Mike Metcalf has made his living building houses that have become homes to dozens of families. But the first home he ever built began as his seven-year marriage came to an end.

After Mike retired from the Air Force, he and his wife started construction on a house in the country. "It was during this time that she served me the papers. My wife had been dating a man she met at work. She was around that man more than she was around me."

Shocked and hurt, Mike tried desperately to hold on to his greatest accomplishment—his two boys, Josh and Nicholas, who were ages three and six. "I went to a lawyer who said, 'No, you're going to lose anyway. Just give them up.'" Feeling lost, lonely, and confused, Mike took the lawyer's advice despite his longing to be with Josh and Nicholas every chance he could.

His defeat mirrored that of so many fathers. "I wanted custody, but only saw them every Wednesday, every other weekend, and several times a year for a week or two."

Mike regrets taking his lawyer's advice to give up easily because it wasn't easy being away from his sons. He passes on his hard-earned wisdom to other single parents. "Fight back. You could never spend too much time with them. I just love my kids."

Shortly after the divorce, Mike moved into a small apartment. "I had a couple of folding chairs, TV trays, and a mattress. That's all I had," but "I had Christmas with [the boys]."

A loving father, Mike "wanted to make those days count." That first Christmas after the divorce, he and his boys filled their tiny apartment—not with toys, but with the love of a father for his sons.

"We went out to the country and chopped down a tree. It wasn't a real tree you know, just a scrappy-looking green tree." No ornaments, no lights, and no star, they took pieces from a game called "Barrel of Monkeys." "We decorated the tree with those little red plastic monkeys. They never forgot that. It was a good Christmas."

Following in their father's footsteps, both boys enlisted in the Air Force, but whenever they come home Mike, Josh, and Nicholas continue to monkey around.

After finishing his first home, Mike's construction company flourished. He remarried a few years later to a lovely woman named Theresa. They were blessed with twin boys, Andrew and Matthew, talented athletes who play basketball, baseball, and football. Mike's successful business allows him to stay at home so that he can go to every game and never miss a practice.

7 ED SHADID –
PROTECTING KIDS FROM CONFLICT

As a spinal care surgeon and city councilman, Dr. Ed Shadid is committed to improving the quality of life for the people of Oklahoma City. Divorced in 2004 and the father of three, he feels passionately about empowering single parents to peacefully co-parent their families.

Humble and soft-spoken, Ed leans in to say, "I have quite a few opinions about the family law system." Dr. Shadid believes the courts are "set up to encourage conflict" during the process of divorce.

He also expresses frustration with the financial incentives of the system, "Lawyers aren't paid by service like [they sometimes are] in criminal law. If you get a DUI, you go in and you pay $5,000-10,000. If it takes a month or six months to settle your case, that's what you pay. In family law, you pay by the hour. So the more hours, the more conflict, the more letters to write, the more court hearings, the more hours get billed." The consequences are devastating both financially and emotionally.

"Now I'm not saying it's just the lawyers. Unfortunately, there's a financial incentive to minimize time with one parent. The system financially rewards how much time is spent in each home. Generally, the father is paying child support to the mother. The more time the child is spending with the mother, the more child support she will receive. Conversely, the less time that is allotted with the father, the more he has to pay." The dynamic causes some dads to be pushed almost completely out of the picture.

Whether rejected, wounded, minimized, or attacked, "for some fathers the emotional pain is too hurtful. So they disengage from their child's life. It's easier to get married and start a new family." Dr. Shadid chose to stay involved because there was nothing worse to him than losing a meaningful relationship with his children.

Speaking about his own family, Dr. Shadid says, "We divide up the weekends, and we divide up the weekdays. We do one-on-one time. We have three children, so maybe I take one and the other two stay with her. That's the thing about single parenting. It makes it even harder to spend one-on-one time with your kids. It can be painful when we've just divided Christmases, really painful. It's sad, and it's just missing things. The first time that they were able to ride a bike without help, and the first time..." his voice quietly trails off into the reminiscence of many lost firsts.

Regardless of the difficulty, the councilman advises, "Parents of divorce have got to find ways to minimize conflict" because "the thing that most injures children in divorce is conflict."

During divorce "the parents are not necessarily in a healthy state." They are angry, yet "anger is a secondary emotion. Anger is never by itself. It's always driven by a primary emotion which is hurt or fear or the loss of control. I don't think I've met somebody going through divorce that wasn't hurt or fearful. And so the propensities for that hurt and fear and loss of control to be expressed as anger is high. To put people in a public courtroom setting amplifies all those emotions. It feeds the conflict which then harms the child."

His proposed solution is to "Keep the parents out of the courtroom and get them in a room with skilled mediators. Ultimately my divorce was settled with the help of a skillful mediator. You've got to get the parents out of the family law system to allow them healing and to allow the conflict to diminish. Another tool that I think is very important is parent coordinators. After the resolution or after you've settled the case, you can have a parent coordinator whose job is to try to meet with the parents and settle conflict without the conflict going back to the courts. They can be appointed by the court. A lot of times they are current or ex-judges, attorneys, or mediators. They have been shown to be very effective at minimizing conflict."

When asked about his ex-wife, Dr. Shadid says, "I don't like to say ex-wife because we are co-parents. Now we are co-parents and friends." The couple goes so far as to take family vacations together so that their children can create special memories with both parents. While few things can be as stressful as traveling, these co-parents have learned how to keep it copasetic. If there's one thing they've succeeded in, Dr. Shadid will tell you, "Deena and I nailed it by shielding them from conflict. We really did that well, and we are the beneficiaries of that."

Despite his seemingly perfect answers, Dr. Ed Shadid reminds us that it's "trial and error. I've got a graduate degree in making mistakes, but [the key is] learning from those mistakes. Everything I've done right I learned by doing wrong first."

8 TRACEY GIVENS—
THE PROTECTOR

"A good parent loves her children, but a great parent puts her children's needs before her own."

–Tracey Givens

Stories of betrayal often tickle our ears and curl our toes, but Tracey Givens doesn't tell hers.

After ten years of marriage, her husband broke his vows, but don't look for scandalous details here.

Tracey can't protect her boys from the pain of a broken home, but at least she will do what she can to protect the relationship they have with their father.

"My job as a parent should be about what's best for them, not what feels good at the moment," she says. "I don't tell my kids negative things about their dad because I don't want to change their relationship with him. He is a good father. If they can have both parents, they should. It's more about what's best for them."

A child of divorce herself, Tracey was most devastated by the fact that her two sons, Jordan and Jacob, only three and five years old at the time her marriage ended, would have to go through the pain that she had suffered.

She didn't need anyone to tell her the dangers of parental alienation. She already knew what many single parents learn too late: that both parents are part of a child's identity and insulting a parent damages the child, too. She also understood that a child needs both parents if at all possible.

"It's really important for kids to have that foundation if you can have both parents, especially for boys with their fathers. I just think it's so important for them to have whatever relationship they can with their dad. It's real easy to get in that 'me' mode and fight back because you're hurt. But ever since I've had kids, I've been focused on raising them as best as I can."

So she refuses to let her husband's behavior damage his relationship with their sons.

Far from bitter, she chooses to focus on the positive. "I've always said, whenever you go through a difficult time, use it. Use it for something positive. I have always felt like God put me in this position so that eventually I could help other people who have gone through something similar. I feel like I'm now at a breaking point where I can jump to the other side—helping people get through the really raw part."

For those still in the "raw part," she encourages them to look to the future, "Try not to be in the moment!"—a stark contrast from the message of so many today living only for the pleasure of the moment. But for Tracey, in the darkest moments of her life, not being in the moment was the only way to get through. "Focus on the good times, and don't get caught up in the stress. Find people you can talk to. Pray."

Toward that end, she encourages single moms to seek support like she found at the Single Parent Support Network. "I love this group so much that now I don't think I can ever not be single," she jokes.

Many single parents suffer with exhaustion from never being able to spend time apart from their kids. Tracey believes "the hardest thing about being a single parent is being *away from* my kids. I worry about them when they are not with me. I can't help them when they are gone."

Tracey defines successful parenting as unselfishness, "I purposely take them to do volunteer work," she says. "I want them to learn how to give to other people and teach them that the stuff isn't what matters. It's people that matter. I hope they live life that way. Kids learn by example. You can talk to them all day long, but they are going to pick up how you live. So I try to live the best way I can around them because I want them to mirror that. I want to be that influence for them."

Even if that means keeping her mouth shut.

9 JENNIFER McCAIN—
THE GOOD GIRL LEARNS GRACE

Today, Jennifer McCain is the kind of parent we all aspire to be. She teaches her daughter to work hard, to save her money, to budget, to give to the less fortunate, to memorize Scripture, to be environmentally conscious, to eat healthy. She's the Mary Poppins of parenting, practically perfect in every way.

But over a decade ago, her husband unexpectedly moved away leaving her and her daughter behind, an experience that shook her identity to its core.

Jennifer met her husband at Texas Christian University, and they started dating in graduate school. They had been married for seven years and were living in Seattle with their two-year-old daughter Alex when he told her of his decision to move. "Two weeks later, he loaded up the car and our dog and drove away," Jennifer remembers.

"I never imagined I would be a single mom," explains Jennifer. "I never imagined I would be divorced. No one in my family has ever been divorced. I married someone I had known for years. I had met his family. He seemed like a stable person. He had never been married before. There wasn't some indicator that looking back, I can say, 'I should have seen that.'"

"I went through an identity crisis," Jennifer says of the first year after the divorce. "I had been a good girl growing up. I had done all the things you were supposed to and not done the things you're not supposed to. I had always been successful: at school, at church, at leadership positions. I remember vividly thinking, 'God can't use me now. I'm divorced. I failed. God will never be able to use me.'"

But through the process of healing, "I really came to know what the word 'grace' meant, that I didn't have to be perfect to have God's love and God's concern for me. I had grown up in church. I had all head knowledge. I believed in God's omnipotence and omniscience, but I did not get the 'love' part. There was a lot of pride in who I was."

"Starting to understand grace gave me so much more empathy for people who had made big mistakes. You know what, I could have just as easily made those mistakes, but God still had a plan for me. I grew a ton. I really learned to trust God. Before, I didn't really have to trust him because everything was going okay on my own."

Within weeks of her husband leaving, God told Jennifer to return to Oklahoma, where she'd grown up and where her parents still lived. "It was the only time in my life when I thought I truly heard God's voice, not a nudging. I felt he was saying, 'Go home. Go back to Norman. I will take care of you and Alex.'"

Within the first three months in Norman, she was teaching three Bible studies at her old home church. "People were more welcoming than I ever could have imagined. Our congregation doesn't have a culture of shunning people, but I was surprised by the number of people, not just my friends, who took me aside one-on-one and who shared that they had been divorced and encouraged me. That was what I needed to hear—that my life was not over now that I was a single mom."

"During that first difficult year I often wondered, 'What was God going to use me for now that I messed up?' They really helped me to see that this is one more thing that he could use to help me reach people I couldn't reach before. A few years later, I taught a 'Rebuilding When Your Relationship Ends' workshop for those going through a divorce. There were ministry opportunities that I never would have been involved in otherwise that helped me to feel that God was going to use me."

"A friend from church shared II Corinthians 1: 3-5 with me. Through it I could see that God was using a horrible time—all my pain and suffering—for some benefit. Even if I wasn't the one who would benefit, he would use it for others and not let it go to waste. That gave me confidence. I was in too much pain to see any good for me, but I would say 'God, I'm going to trust you that others will benefit from this.' I finally got to the point where I could see that, not just trust it, but see that evidence."

God was also teaching Jennifer to trust for their physical needs as she and Alex struggled to make ends meet.

"I remember vividly one time, I needed new contacts. But I didn't have insurance or the money. That same week at Bible study, someone left a card in my Bible with $100 in it. There are just so many examples of God being faithful."

Jennifer recounts one especially memorable example of God's faithfulness when she was considering whether or not to participate in her church's Operation Santa Claus program by selecting a name of a needy child to buy presents for off a Christmas tree like they had in years past.

As a single mom, she thought, "This year *my* child needs to be on that tree."

But then she realized giving to someone less fortunate was, "as much for us as for that child. We need to be obedient and do that, and I need to be an example to my child."

That same afternoon, her dad unexpectedly offered to take her and her daughter grocery shopping. "I just need to do that," he said.

Jennifer sobbed tears of relief, "I just committed $50 this morning to buy presents for another child, and I really didn't know how I was going to pay my bills and buy my groceries this month."

"There are so many examples of how God was telling me if I would trust him, if I would be obedient to what he was telling me to do, he would take care of the details."

Healing didn't come easily though.

"I don't say this lightly," says Jennifer. "But there was spiritual warfare going on in my mind during that first year." She felt the pull between the "truth that God was trying to help me remember versus what Satan was whispering in my ear." She typed out four pages of Bible verses about her identity in Christ and taped them outside her shower's glass walls. "I would read those everyday while I was taking my shower and brushing my teeth."

"One that stuck with me more than any of the others was Jeremiah 29:11. God has a future for me. There is a future. I don't know what it is, but it is good. God has something planned for me."

Verses about Jesus interceding for us, like Job 16:19-21, also gave her great comfort "because there were so many times I was praying, that I was so upset that I couldn't even form a sentence. I knew if I was down on my knees, crying my eyes out, Jesus was my intercessor. That was comforting to me. Isaiah 41:10,13 tells of God taking hold of our right hand, and upholding us with His right hand. I imagined not holding God's hand and walking side by side, but Him holding my hands and walking with me as you would a baby. A parent can look where the baby is going, and direct and protect them. That really helped me. I don't have to know where I'm going. I don't have to do this in my own strength. He's got me. He's holding on to me. That was definitely comforting."

One of the many who have benefitted from Jennifer's faith journey is her daughter Alex. Jennifer tells of how after her father left, Alex started waking up every night, screaming and panicked with night terrors. "I would sing her a little song to calm her, 'The Lord is my light and my salvation, whom shall I fear?' from Psalm 27. I'd sing it to her, and then she'd sing it back to me." Years later, that is still Alex's favorite verse, and her mother will hear her singing it to herself when she is low. "She believes," says Jennifer. "She knows even if everything is falling apart, there is nothing to be afraid of."

10 AMY JONES–
THE SURVIVOR

Psalms 126:5 – "They that sow in tears shall reap in joy." (KJV)

Amy Jones never knew the power of God's love until she experienced abuse and cancer. The abuse came first.

Amy was married to her high school sweetheart for ten years before, one day, she finally drew the line. Her husband never came home from the bar on the day of her oldest daughter's seventh birthday. "He wanted to live like he was single even though he was married. He didn't bring anything to the table. He didn't hold a job. He wasn't a good father," she says of her decision to divorce.

Even more than the physical abuse she would later suffer, the emotional abuse she endured for years left permanent scars, causing her to question her worth. "My ex-husband and his family always beat me down," remembers Amy. "They tore me down to build themselves up. His very best asset was making me look dumb. All those years that I gave up so much, worked three jobs, tried so hard—and I still didn't believe I was good enough. I didn't believe I had done a good job."

But when Amy made the decision to get divorced and never looked back, her troubles really began. Her husband, who had never been physically abusive before, starting stalking her. "He broke into the house and stole all my clothes. He wouldn't give them back until I did what he wanted. Another time, he threw a brick through my car window and then broke each window with a golf club." In a small town, he was able to talk his way out of the first restraining order she got. Another time, he ran her car off the road with one of her daughters inside.

Amy found that while there seemed to be resources available for lower-income women in abusive relationships, she couldn't find support among her peers. "No one would do anything about it. Because we were technically still married, he wouldn't get in trouble. I just had to stand there and take it. People turned their heads and pretended like it didn't happen."

Tearfully she recalls the first Christmas after she and her two daughters left. "I told him that he and his family could have the girls whenever he wanted, but I wasn't going to celebrate Christmas with him. He broke in the house. We looked up, and he was just standing there. Then he started picking ornaments off the tree and broke them one at a time. The ornaments were my special collection that my seven-year-old daughter Madison adored. Madison pleaded with him to stop. 'Those are going to be mine one day, Daddy,' she begged. Four-year-old Molly crawled to a corner and cried. Finally, I agreed to let him stay. I felt I had no choice."

"He used material things and money to force me to have a relationship with him because that was all he had control over," says Amy, echoing the desperate plight of so many women trapped in abusive relationships. For years after their divorce, her ex-husband would still continue to try to manipulate her and threaten, beat up, or slash the tires of anyone she dated.

Still, Amy persevered. She was even living her dream of running a successful diner in her hometown of El Reno, Oklahoma, when she received a surprising diagnosis. At 37-years-old, two days before Madison's sixteenth birthday, she discovered she had stage-four breast cancer.

She can now see God's plan of redemption through the cancer. "The blessing of having cancer was that I got to make everything right in my life that was wrong. What I learned when I was dying was that people really did like me, that they cared for me. I also realized that God had a plan for me. He has a perfect plan, and His timing is perfect for everything. I had lost that," says Amy.

Within four weeks, she had chemotherapy and two surgeries, then eight more weeks of chemo before a double mastectomy. She lost all her hair. Her daughters helped her shave her head when it started falling out. She cried and sweat red from the "red devil" poison doctors gave her to try to kill the cancer cells. Unable to work, she was forced to close her diner.

But joy often comes out of sorrow. Her very sweetest memories are of her girls lying in bed with her when she was sick. "I knew they loved me. I knew they cared about me. Nothing is sweeter than when you are sick and your children want to come lay with you."

"I told them I didn't want my illness to change their lives. This was an important time in their lives, and I didn't want it to affect that." Specifically, Amy didn't want her sickness to affect Madison's chances at an athletic scholarship. "I knew from the time she was seven that she would be playing college ball," Amy says of her daughter, who became the captain of the University of Kansas women's softball team. Madison was named one of the five best softball players in the country, and she will be the first college graduate in their family.

In the midst of her sickness, though, Amy found all that she had been looking for. "Until I got cancer, I wasn't real religious. I only prayed when I needed God," she says. Believing you are dying has a way of deepening one's thoughts about God.

Now, Amy sees God's plan for each stage of her life, even the hardest times. She especially sees his provision in her new husband. "He married me when I was bald and had no breasts. That's God," Amy chuckles. She believes that during her ten years as a single parent she was trying so hard to be strong and independent for her daughters that she wasn't vulnerable enough to have a meaningful and transforming relationship with a partner. "I was trying so hard to show them we didn't need a man for anything," she recalls. The cancer changed that.

Not only has her new husband provided for Amy and cared for her following her illness, he also broke the pattern of her ex-husband's abuse, refusing to be intimidated by his threats, and has begun to help Amy heal her emotional scars from decades of verbal abuse.

This knight in shining armor came from his own tale of heartache though. His daughter played softball on the same team with Amy's oldest daughter. His wife left him for a lesbian relationship with their female softball coach. Initially, Amy helped him gain custody of his four children by writing the court a letter detailing how the coach had previously propositioned her. "I wrote the letter in longhand in bed just before my mastectomy because I didn't want to die without helping him," says Amy.

Their friendship turned into a fairy tale romance for which Amy gives God all the credit. She believes God used it even to help her survive cancer. Two mothers of other girls on their softball team had cancer at the same time, but only Amy survived. "They were such wonderful women. I wonder why they didn't make it and I did," Amy ponders. She thinks part of the reason is that when she got married, "I finally got to rest."

Their blended family now consists of two parents, six teenagers, and a dog living in a big beautiful historic home in their hometown of El Reno. Amy now says, "I thought I was a good parent before. I'm trying to become a great parent now. A good parent is okay with status quo. You look at what society says, and you do that. Now I know I need to allow my children to be who they are—no matter what. I'm willing to be criticized now because I got a second chance to be a parent. I'm going to be the best parent I can be. I would do anything for them. We're a family. I'm trying to figure out who I am because what makes great kids is having parents who know who they are."

Amy knows who she is now. She is a good mom. She is a good wife. She is a cancer survivor. And she will soon be an entrepreneur again re-opening Amy's Downtown Diner in El Reno, Oklahoma.

11 SUSAN LEONARD –
BROKEN HEARTS DON'T ALWAYS STAY BROKEN

Susan Leonard didn't marry her high school sweetheart. She didn't rush into marriage or motherhood by accident or impetuousness. She waited until she met the love of her life at thirty-three and had her first and only daughter Raye at thirty-five.

But unfortunately, the loves of our lives don't always love us back.

So after caring for her husband through twenty surgeries in three and a half years, she was heartbroken and devastated when he left her and six-year-old Raye. "He got addicted to his pain killers," said Susan, "and you can probably write the rest of the story without me even telling you."

But broken hearts don't always stay broken.

"I'm so much more joyful than I ever thought I could be," marvels Susan. "I have a deep sense of love and satisfaction down in the pit of my being. I can't believe that this incredible creature is my daughter."

Susan understands why some parents just aren't up to the task of single parenting. Even as a disciplined, high achiever with a supportive family, she says, "It's the hardest thing I have ever done in my entire life to raise Raye on my own." But as her daughter now heads to the University of Tulsa on a scholarship, she holds out hope for those who persevere to the end, "I don't have one regret for any sacrifice I made."

After her divorce, Susan began to date. Having heard all the studies about young girls who are raised without fathers becoming promiscuous, she wanted to provide a good stepfather for Raye. But despite the loneliness of living in "the land of the married" in Yukon, Oklahoma, she chose to stop after a few relationships. "There wasn't enough time."

She believes the two most important things that single parents should do are to spend a lot of time with their kids and to communicate. "Quantity is more important than 'quality' time. You can't really pick your quality time. It happens in snippets here and there. You've got to pay attention and talk to them daily."

She admits it was her daughter, though, who taught her about communication. "Kids make you so much better than you ever think you can be," offers Susan. "Raye has taught me to be more careful of people's feelings, to think before I speak, to be more kind, to learn how to apologize and to listen, to control my temper better. She is wise beyond her years."

Maintaining a career and supporting her family was "a huge struggle" for Susan. When you divorce you are "broken and broke," according to Susan, whose divorce attorney hands out bankruptcy attorney cards as well. She refused to go down the bankruptcy route because she "didn't want to feel guilt about that" in addition to everything else. Working in sales, Susan depended on bonuses and commissions to make ends meet. She went to work early, stayed through lunch, and worked as "furious and fast" as she could so that she could have evenings with her daughter.

Susan and Raye have soared high above the challenges of single parenting. An overachiever like her mother, Raye graduated as valedictorian of her high school class, but Susan considers her greatest parenting success to be Raye's independence. Teaching life skills isn't easy. "It's hard work," warns Susan. "It's really hard, but you have to do it. I didn't want my daughter to confuse being smart with being able to make a living."

She began giving Raye an allowance at the age of ten for her entertainment expenses. She slowly increased the amount and the time between payments until Raye was responsible for all of her own expenses. She taught her to make a budget, requiring her to save 10%, invest 10%, and give 10% away. When she began to drive, Susan told her that she would pay for her gas and insurance if Raye would do all the errands.

"It takes a lot of discipline. You've got to explain it, make it real, and let them learn the hard lessons," explains Susan. Those hard lessons have taken root, and Susan and Raye both now enjoy their hard-won fruit of maturity, generosity, and responsibility. Susan tells with pride how Raye took the initiative to save her money after a church mission trip in order to pay the $250 required for an eighth grade girl in Mexico to attend high school.

Faith didn't play a role in Susan's life before her divorce, but the "devastation brought me to my knees." Susan confesses, "I knew I couldn't make it on my own." She was influenced by her neighbors who invited her daughter to church. Never condemning Susan, they lived their faith simply. She says she "never had an epiphany moment," but just "liked what I saw" in her neighbors and grew in her own faith as she began to read the Bible and pray daily.

Now she says faith is the single most important element in thriving as a single parent. "If I didn't have my relationship with God, my daily prayer, and my relationship with my church, I could not have done nearly as well. It keeps you sane. It gives you health—how people could care for you and your children so much. That's what amazes me about church—how all these other people get so entangled in your child's life, and they truly care. So when you can't do it anymore, they step in and fill the gap."

photo by Bryan Crump

12 DEENA GIRDNER–
MENDED LITTLE HEARTS

"Will I ever be happy again?" wondered Deena Girdner, after the tragic death of her fiancé just three weeks before their wedding. "I couldn't find a smile to save my life. I had accepted that I would never be happy again," she recalls.

Now, less than two years after Mike's death, she is helping others to find their way while she is still searching for hers. Deena found the inspiration to serve others through her own painful loss.

"I was four months pregnant when Mike passed away, and to say the least, I was completely devastated losing the man I loved while carrying our baby." On July 4, 2011, he fell off a golf cart in a freak accident while they were at the lake. "He had stood up and held onto the top and either lost his footing or lost his grip." Deena was still back at the cabin. "I never even saw him. By the time I made it there, the ambulance was already taking him." Deena never saw Mike again.

"Everyone thought he was going to be fine." In hindsight, she remembers asking, "'Why did you call off the medi-flight? He needs the medi-flight!' The EMT looked at me and shook his head. I thought 'Oh, so it must not be that bad. They are going to fix him in the hospital.' That's what I remember thinking, that it's not that bad, not that it wasn't necessary."

"When we got to the hospital Mike was declared dead upon arrival." The fall caused Mike to hit his head right at the brain stem, killing him instantly at the age of forty-one. While it was the end for Mike, it was just the beginning for Deena.

Three days before Christmas, the young mother found herself back in a hospital again. "Macey Rene was born, and my life was forever changed. Not only am I still grieving the loss of Mike, but within minutes of delivering Macey, she was taken away. The nurse kept saying, 'Something is not right.' I just kept asking, 'Why? Will she live or not?'" The first time Deena got to hold her newborn child, she was twenty-three days old.

Macey, named after her father, Mike Macey, was born with a very rare heart condition: tetralogy of fallot with pulmonary atresia. About 1 in 100,000 babies are born with the condition. Two weeks later, Macey had her first open-heart surgery. "It was absolutely the scariest day of my life." As the doctors opened up Macey's heart, Deena's started to close.

"Being in the hospital was really tough. There were all these decisions, and I just got really angry and thought, 'Where is Mike, I need him.'"

During their four-week stay in the hospital while Macey recovered, they also found out she had a ventricular septal defect (VSD), a hole in the wall that separates the right and left ventricles of the heart. Then a few months later, she was diagnosed with pyloric stenosis, another condition that usually is diagnosed in boys between two and four weeks old and occurs in 1 in 1,000 births.

"You have no idea the level of stress. You have all of these life-changing decisions to make, and I was the one who had to make these decisions. I was the only one. That's been one of my main things since Mike has been gone, is not being able to make a decision. With stress and grief and loss, the front part of your brain, the decision-making part, becomes so clouded."

Overwhelmed by the enormity of the life-threatening decisions she had to make for Macey, Deena eventually felt paralyzed to make any decision at all. She tells this story to illustrate how severe it became. "I sat at this stop sign the other day and I was like, 'Just pick.' I go the wrong way all the time. You know, just go left, if it's wrong, turn around. I sat there, and I sat there. It was almost four or five minutes. A car came behind me and honked its horn twice before I finally moved. I moved forward across the intersection, and then I pulled over to the side of the road because I still wouldn't make up my mind on which way. I was like, 'Deena, just pick a way! If it's wrong, it's wrong!' But I could not make myself drive in any way."

With the support of family and friends, Deena has begun moving forward, one decision at a time. "Mike's family has been so supportive through all of this." In addition, Deena's mom comes to watch Macey twice a week so Deena can run errands because "even though Macey is healed and doing good now, she is not able to go to a daycare for at least two years," or be exposed to a lot of germs due to the fact that her immune system is still weaker than most.

Deena is using her pain to help others. "There is this group called the Mended Little Hearts Club. It's part of the National Heart Association. They have meetings once a month. It's a small support group. There are moms who you can talk to and call and ask questions." Deena joined the group and, after completing a volunteer class, is now helping others like her. "I have met with four different moms now. I see me in them, that fear and the deer-in-the-headlights, someone-just-tell-me-what-is-going-on type thing, and the stress level!"

Deena literally stands in hospital rooms alongside other parents of infant heart patients as they receive critical information from doctors about their own children. She offers others the support she never had.

"Macey will always have a heart condition," and Deena will always be considered a "heart mom," but with time they have both begun to heal. "While this is not the life that I would have planned for myself, losing my best friend, Mike, and having a baby with a heart condition, God has sent me on this path. While it has been the hardest time of my life, I love that

Macey looks just like her daddy, so I get to see a little piece of Mike every single day. What makes me smile now is Macey."

photo by Stacy Becker

13 DENNSECIA ROBINSON— GOD'S DELAYS ARE NOT HIS DENIALS

"There is no better than adversity. Every defeat, every heartbreak, every loss, contains its own seed, its own lesson on how to improve your performance next time." – Malcolm X

Dee Robinson has weathered many trials, but her joy cuts through a room like sunlight through the clouds.

With her gentle smile and warm spirit, she immediately catches your attention, but even more impressive is her eleven-year-old son with his quiet self-confidence and impeccable manners. At first glance, you would never guess that either of these beautiful souls had known the hardships that they have worked to overcome.

Today she speaks of character, praying with Justice each morning, and teaching him to "put on the full armor of God" as her aunt taught her years ago. She only regrets that she wasn't able to "muster the strength to walk away from the disappointments of past relationships the moment they began to sour." Having experienced domestic violence herself and having lost two cousins to it she says, "You know it's time [to go] when the pain of staying is greater than [the pain of] leaving."

Voted most likely to succeed in her high school senior class, Dee attended college and was struggling to break the chains of her own childhood, having been raised by a single parent, when she became pregnant.

"Society says that you have to have a two-parent home to successfully raise your children. I made a vow to myself not to place a man above my child. You don't have to have a man to complete yourself."

T.S. Elliot once said, "The end is where we start from." Dee knows firsthand about starting afresh, like many other Americans that experienced corporate downsizing, Dee found herself unemployed. She adamantly searched for employment for over a year and a half. Through the many lows and times of hopelessness during her journey, tears often conveyed what words could not.

"As difficult as it was, I learned some of life's greatest lessons," says Dee. "So many times, the independence that we develop as single mothers often becomes both a blessing and a curse. We become so consumed with doing everything on our own that when we do need help, our pride prohibits us from asking. It is as if asking for help is interpreted as a sign of weakness. It's as if asking for help says that you are feeble or incompetent. I never wanted to be anyone's charity case."

"Yet, when you are all out of options, God is still faithful and sends a ram in the bush. God has blessed me immensely with so many rams in my darkest hours via friends, family, strangers, and spiritual family." From the difficult times, Dee learned that "starting over is part of the journey. It's not over until God says it's done."

Good parents rise to the occasion, but great ones go above and beyond. During a time when Dee could have become consumed with her own challenges, she turned all of her attention to creating a better life for her son. She has been a dedicated leader in her community and consistently engaged to enrich the life of her son via community programs and positive role models. Justice had a thirty-six month wait to be matched with a mentor, but now has both a loving and remarkable Big Brother and an equally remarkable Big Sister. Today, she says, "If you don't go through the test then you won't have a testimony."

Dee's vision for her family is hanging on a dream board in her kitchen with photos and words representing her dreams for her son, financial security, and a debt-free home. The board reminds her both of her hope for the future and of her many answered prayers.

Receiving the Kevin Durant Empowerment Grant through Single Parent Support Network enabled Dee to start her own business as a Mary Kay Consultant, another dream from her board that is now a reality! Dee believes that "just because you were a victim, doesn't mean you can't be a victor."

Dee has bold dreams for her son. She dreams of him breaking statistics and stereotypes, shattering the generational curses that have plagued their family, and charting his own path instead of following the ones he's seen taken.

"Never give up," she encourages other single parents. "God's delays are not his denials."

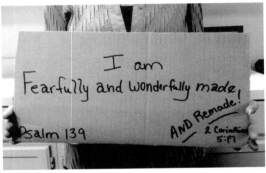

14 JENNIFER M. –
NO HOME IS BROKEN
WITH GOD IN IT

Words of encouragement flow from Jennifer like a refreshing stream. The petite redhead with clear blue eyes has known crippling pain, but now you can't stop her from sharing her joy and hope for the future. "These are the best years of my life!" she exclaims.

"Statistics without help is just discouragement," she says of the stereotypes about single parent families. "Encouraging single moms is what I'm all about."

Only four years ago, Jennifer's sixteen-year marriage ended in a breathtaking moment when she accidentally uncovered evidence of her husband's secret life. In spite of her shock, anger, and hurt, she tried to protect her young daughters Joey (five) and Kyrie (two) from both their father's actions and her own despair. "God gave me clarity that whatever I might do in the way of vindictiveness would be short term for me and short term for my husband, but long term for my kids."

"I could not grieve on a day-to-day basis. I would come home from work, put a movie on for the girls, and go in the bathroom and sob on the floor. When you've been married as long as I had, it was suffocating to have that support and emotional connection gone. I would look at the future, and it looked like not much fun—bleak, hard work, kids to take care of, and never enough of anything: time or money. I know now that's not true, but I couldn't see it then. Fear takes us to the extent of the negative possibility, and doesn't see God with us."

Now, on the other side of the most painful part of her journey, she wants to tell other single parents, "God is working where you don't even know. My story is all about how God was and is in it."

Formerly reserved and insecure, Jennifer is now a leader at Celebrate Recovery, a Christ-centered recovery program with her church, and takes every opportunity to encourage others. She tells of God's faithfulness in providentially providing friends and a counselor to walk with her through her darkest hours after her divorce. She gratefully recalls the sixteen people from her church family who showed up to help her and her children move to a smaller house.

She shares how God mysteriously handled even the smallest details. Like when she had tearfully sent her lawyer the $800 her mother had given her for bunk beds for her daughters. The next week, someone gave them bunk beds unsolicited and another friend mentioned in passing having twin mattresses they didn't need. "They didn't even know we needed them," she marvels.

"I was headed down a very dark path," she remembers. "But God is close to the brokenhearted. When I could not reach out, he brought what I needed to me."

"You have to get to a place where you are so miserable that you are ready to change. I had a lot of pride that had to get out of the way. I thought I had tried to live a godly life, but that was only on a surface level. When you are a single parent and have two kids to take care of, pride has a way of going. When I got miserable enough, I realized I can't do it on my own. That's not a bad place to be; that's the best place to be."

All her life, Jennifer had "based her identity in people, places, and things and was miserable." She even based her view of God on her relationships with people thinking he would "abandon, betray, or reject her." She now counts her greatest success in life as discovering her identity in Christ.

"My relationship with Christ has grounded me, given me a center; whereas, before, I felt I had no control over my life. I was just blown about by whatever circumstances. But now I know that even if the unthinkable happens, it is going to be used for my good, and that God is going to get me through that."

She encourages other single parents to "just take the steps toward God, and He will get you there. It's a process, not an event."

After discovering her identity in Christ, she views her second greatest success as breaking the pattern of negative behaviors for her girls and sparing them unnecessary suffering. "The law of generations works both ways—negative and positive. My children have been watching me walk through this and not let it ruin me. And they know why. It does not matter what [their father] has done. What matters is what we are doing. We pray together every night. Joey is growing to be such a godly child. I'm such a better person now, not at all the bleak picture I had."

When her daughter was crying on the floor "wanting daddy to be out of time out," Jennifer recalls comforting her, "I told her this is not the picture of how we thought it would be. But God was with us before, and he is with us now, and we will be okay."

"It took me a long time to get past that idea that we are not a real family. I would hear these statistics that my kids were 'at risk' because there was no father in the home, and I would think, 'Why even try?' But statistics are the world's view of my family, not God's view. Before—that was the broken home—with my husband's deception, with our emotional baggage, with me feeling invisible. Today, I am determined that statistics will not define me or my children. No home is broken with God in it."

15 GOVERNOR MARY FALLIN—
BALANCING FAITH, FAMILY, AND CAREER

No one would question that Oklahoma Governor Mary Fallin has an impressive resume. She has served for over twenty-three years in state and national politics, setting records and breaking glass ceilings along the way. She says her most rewarding job, however, is being a mother to her daughter Christina and her son Price.

Starting with knocking on doors while she was pregnant with Price as a state house candidate, Gov. Fallin has seamlessly combined the roles of parent and politician since the beginning of her political career. Perpetually poised and polished, Fallin seems to keep it all in balance, while shattering stereotypes, challenging political insiders, and blazing a trail for future generations.

She was not only Oklahoma's first female lieutenant governor, but Oklahoma's first republican lieutenant governor. She gave up her twelve-year post in 2006 to win a coveted, hotly contested Congressional seat. But after four years, she returned to her home state to win election as Oklahoma's first female governor in 2010.

"No one ever wants to end up being a single parent," says Governor Fallin. But when her fourteen-year marriage ended suddenly in a very public way, Mary kept her faith in God. "Faith has always played a big role in my life," she says. She found comfort in the words of Proverbs 3:5-6, "Trust in the Lord with all your heart, and lean not on your own understanding and God will guide and direct your steps [paraphrase]." She adds, "I had to trust that there would be a good plan, and it would all turn out okay. And it has."

Despite her long list of political accomplishments, Governor Fallin maintains that her greatest success story is "walking through the challenging times being a single parent and walking by faith—trusting in God to get me through, to provide the courage and strength to move forward with my career, but also teaching me the priorities of life—my faith and family, and then my career—and to be able to do all three successfully."

"My message to single parents is that you can be whatever you want to be. You can still have a great life. You can still have a great family. Families just take on different forms at different times."

"Being a single parent isn't easy," says Governor Fallin who had to balance caring not only for her two children but for her elderly mom as well. "I had a busy job, a busy life, but my first priority was being a good mom to both my children, to let them know that even though our family was a single-parent family, we would still have a great family. I was actively engaged in both of their lives. I put their events on my schedule first. I made sure I attended as much of those as possible. I would volunteer. We had lots of kids over to our house. We had sleepovers. I took them and their friends on vacations, to concerts, to the state fair, to various events, trying to spend time with them and their friends."

"When I became a single mom, I was worried I wouldn't be able to continue my political career," admits Governor Fallin whose campaign theme was "Faith, Family, and Values." She continues, "Sometimes people can be judgmental, but what I found was that life happens to everyone."

The support of her children, however, was non-negotiable says Gov. Fallin recalling a pivotal conversation they had when she was considering leaving the lieutenant governor's job to run for Congress.

Christina asked, "Have you made a decision [if you're going to run for Congress]? You know, everyone wants you to."

"I just don't think I will," Fallin responded, having at the time decided not to run. "I need to stay here in Oklahoma."

Christina turned around and looked her in the eye and said dramatically, "Mother, we think this is your destiny to run for Congress."

"Destiny—that's a pretty big word for a nineteen-year-old girl," Fallin laughed.

Her son Price interjected, "Well, I'm not sure I want you to go to Congress."

"Why not?" asked Christina.

"Because she drives me around all the time and picks me up from school."

"You're going to be sixteen in a couple of months, so you'll be driving yourself," Christina reminded him.

"Oh, I hadn't thought about that. Okay. Run for Congress. I don't care."

Gov. Fallin laughs as she tells the story but adds, "That was a life-changing moment because I literally would not have run if my kids had not encouraged me to do it."

She wants other parents to know that the most important thing is "letting your children know that you love them unconditionally. I have always let them know they are the first priority in my life, next to my faith. I would always be there for them when they needed me. They knew they had my love no matter what position I held."

"We have a joke between my children and me. I used to tell them, 'You're my favorite boy in the whole world.' Or 'You're my favorite girl in the whole world.' Last Mother's Day, they gave me a card that said, 'You're our favorite mom in the whole world!' As we read it, we all laughed. I guess they never forgot."

Governor Fallin is now serving in the third year of her first term as governor, but during her gubernatorial campaign she says God "brought me the nice surprise" of her current husband Wade Christensen. They began their whirlwind courtship with a date spent riding four hours together on a combine harvesting wheat on his family farm in Thomas, Oklahoma. Five months later, he showed up unexpectedly to propose on a cold, rainy night at the Lincoln Memorial Monument in Washington, D.C. where Fallin was still serving as a member of Congress. They married during her campaign and when she was elected governor, he became Oklahoma's first "First Gentleman."

16 AMY COXON–
CHOOSING TO BE A SINGLE MOM

Most people wouldn't choose single parenthood. But Dr. Amy Coxon, a thirty-six-year-old professional working at the National Institute of Health (NIH) in Washington, D.C. raised $45,000, took months off work, and traveled across the globe to have the privilege of becoming a single mom to her daughter Raya.

When asked what sacrifices she has made as a single parent, Amy draws a blank. Normally quick with an answer to every question, the former college professor is stumped. She finally says, "I haven't thought that I've sacrificed anything. I've gained a richness to my life that I never knew could exist."

Amy's journey through international adoption was far from smooth, but she was convinced from the beginning that God led her on this path. Starting with a mission trip working with kids from war-torn Kosovo, God used a particular little girl to start an ache in her heart. "She could not even look at me," said Amy. "It took me almost an hour on my knees to get her to respond in any way. I still have her impression in my head because it was so sad all that she had been through."

Despite that experience and the tug in her heart, "For six months, I kept telling God he had the wrong person. I thought, 'I can't do this on my own, and I don't want to.' But it got so bad, I couldn't even hear about international adoption without sobbing."

Submitting to God's leading, she originally sought to adopt from Bulgaria but hit a dead end when adoptions there were closed. The adoption agency asked if she would be willing to adopt an older girl from Kazakhstan. She said, "Send me a picture, and I'll pray about it." When she saw a photo of Raya, "It was instantaneous. I knew I was going to adopt her. It was in my heart. I knew."

To this day, Raya's favorite photo is of their first meeting in the orphanage when Raya was only three years old (on previous page). For months after, they would navigate through the frustrating tangle of third-world agencies and regulations. "It breaks my heart to think of one of our hardest days there. The translator literally had to pry her off of me to take her back to the orphanage. She was beside herself. It was horrible," Amy remembers. Raya would turn four on December 23 before Amy gained custody on Christmas Day. "It was the biggest Christmas present ever. She really is the biggest present I've ever gotten. She is my huge blessing. I tell her that all the time."

Raya seems wise beyond her years. "When she wasn't even five, she thanked me for telling her about Jesus because 'no one in Kazakhstan ever did,'" marvels Amy. "She belongs to God. She is [only] mine to raise. Even her teacher said me, 'She has a depth of understanding of Scripture that none of the other kids in this class, or even most of the kids I've ever had, has had. She ties stuff together, and it makes sense to her.' I look at her and wonder what God is going to do with her life. There is a reason. He knew we were going to be together before He created the earth. I know there is a reason."

She tells of Raya's generous heart, planning for six months what she might do for a birthday or Mother's Day. "Her heart is incredibly tender and incredibly giving. I treasure how much she cares about me and other people." Most recently, nine-year-old Raya tried to surprise her mom by calling her from the bedroom pretending to be someone else asking to meet at a local restaurant "for a business meeting" on her birthday. She later confessed her prank (no surprise to Amy). But she also revealed she had saved up $45 and begged, "I really want to take you out for your birthday." Amy emphasizes, "She does this stuff all the time!"

"I never had any clue that I could love a child so much," says Amy. "Not that I didn't want to get married, but I never felt the huge desperation that everyone [else] felt. It wasn't how I was focused. I was caught up in my career, and that was it. [With Raya] I gained this perspective on what's important, on how much you can love someone else."

If pressed, Amy admits she misses being "more in the thick of things in science" instead of taking a manageable forty-hour-a-week job at NIH so she could spend more time with Raya. "It's not what I did my PhD for, but on the other hand, I'd give up my job tomorrow if I could stay home and home-school Raya."

Amy doesn't take credit for Raya's kindness and tenderness of heart. "It's just her personality," she says. But she does believe in the importance of speaking truth and speaking Scripture into the lives of children. "We opened up that dialogue when she was little." She offers as an example a solution to a known adoption issue, "She will sometimes be very hard on herself. She gets a B, and it's the end of the world. 'I'm horrible. I'm the worst daughter ever,' she'll say. I would tell her, 'You are created in God's image, and you are the daughter of the King of the Universe. You need to believe that because Satan is telling you lies.' I try to speak truth to her about who she is in Christ, and that Jesus died for her and loves her more than I ever can." Another truth from Scripture that Amy likes to share with Raya is "Obey those in authority so that it will go well with you."

Amy tries to encourage other single adoptive parents and to educate the church on single adoption, "I'd love to be able to get a message across that you can be a single mom and have an awesome life! Many parents, single or not, are trying to get away from their kids. It makes me sad because I love spending time with Raya. Parenting is really a blessing from God, and we should see our kids that way, not as a trap to keep us from hanging out with our friends and doing what we want to do."

For those considering single adoption, Amy emphasizes that she felt very clearly called to adoption and you "should be where God wants you to be." For all parents, she reminds us of the heart-breaking truth that we should "cherish our kids as long as we can because they grow up too fast."

17 JOHN ALBAUGH—
THE FATHER WHO REFUSES TO ABANDON HIS CHILDREN

As the chief of staff for a powerful Congressman, John Albaugh had it all—wealth, power, prestige, a beautiful family, a loving wife, and the respect of those around him. He was a deacon in his church, the boss at his work, and had just been named Father of the Year in his community.

Until the day he lost it all.

John will forever view his life in two parts—the time before and the days after the FBI showed up at his door. "We would like to speak with you about a relationship you had with a lobbyist," they said. A chain of events started that day that would ultimately strip him of everything he held dear, including his wife and three children. Caught up in the Jack Abramoff lobbying scandal, John would plead guilty to felony charges of honest services fraud and would lose his reputation, his wealth, his occupation, and ultimately his freedom.

But John's story did not end there. In fact, it had just started.

While he lost everything the world views as success, John is not bitter. He is not depressed. Instead, his big booming laugh has returned, just like it was before the years in Congress slowly squeezed it out of him. In response to questions from concerned friends about how he is doing, he can honestly say, "The joy of the Lord is my strength!" John knows the answer to that question that so many of us secretly wonder, "If we lost it all, would Jesus alone really be enough?" John can now answer with a resounding, "Absolutely!"

Now, John has a heart for those who are broken. He has started a ministry called "Levi's House" to help ex-convicts to re-enter society. He spends his days sharing the good news of God's unconditional love with those who have reached the bottom. John recalls sharing with a prisoner for the first time. Though the prisoner was crying and depressed, "I was able to tell him, 'The Lord has not abandoned you. He didn't leave you when you walked in that door. He still loves you. He cares about you.' Then he started crying because of that. When I left, I started praising God that I had something to share with him because I certainly didn't before. That's for sure."

In addition to losing his professional reputation, his material wealth, many friends, and even his freedom, John also lost his family when his wife filed for divorce on the day he was scheduled to be sentenced.

"It's hard to say that you're glad that divorce happens in your life because of the pain it causes. Let me be clear about that—I'd prefer not be divorced. It's not a positive thing in itself, but I wouldn't be the same person I am today if I hadn't had to go through those struggles."

Recently John was living in a friend's basement and didn't have enough money to do his laundry, but he has what he never had before: the joy of the Lord and the confidence of who He is in Christ. For those who knew him before as a powerful and skillful but arrogant Congressional staffer, the transformation is shocking.

Of all the trials and challenges he has faced, however, becoming "the other parent" to his children has been the most painful.

To other dads whose families have been broken, he offers the advice,

"Understand that this is broken; this is not the way it is supposed to be. Acknowledge that it's painful, but understand that they are still your responsibility. They are still your children. You are still their dad."

"Be consistent in who you are as a person. Circumstances are going to change regardless. Kids can deal with situational change pretty well, but they can't deal with you changing. To the extent you can get along with your spouse, you should. Don't think about finding something or someone else to make the pain go away. Stay in their lives. This season will pass."

"It's a terrible thing to say," says John, but he admits that the pain of not being with his children every day was so gut-wrenching that he was tempted to give up and start over. "You just want to stop the pain in any way you can. It's horribly painful to have that mantle stripped away: to go from being, in my head, a version of super dad, to basically not having any kids."

John chose to stay, face the pain, and find the positive in it. "I've always prayed for my kids, but it's different when you have to say to the Lord, 'Father, I have to trust You to answer these prayers, to put a hedge of protection around them, to keep their hearts safe, and to draw them to You because I'm not there to teach them about You.' You have to really be dependent on God, really calling on God to be true to his character."

John also speaks of the joy of seeing the fruits of those prayers. "When I was in the halfway house, I had a lot of people praying for my kids." During that time, his sixteen-year-old son John went on a mission trip to inner city St. Louis. John was amazed at the changes he saw in his son when he returned, "He's not one to be focused on other people, but his favorite thing that summer was going on that mission trip. Now he wants to go to Africa."

John continues to intercede for his fourteen-year-old daughter Sally. "She's having a really difficult time. That's been very hard on me. She's my little girl." Overhearing her mother's negative conversations during the divorce, however, has "really damaged my relationship with her. My prayer is that the Lord would take that poison out of her heart and our relationship would be restored. I continue in faith to believe that will come about."

Ironically, the entire experience has deepened John's relationship with his own father and given them a connection they never had before. John's parents divorced when he was young, and his father remarried and started another family. John always felt like a stepchild, like a third wheel who didn't belong in that family. "I don't feel that anymore. That's the Lord."

Prior to his conviction, John, a teetotalling Presbyterian deacon who regularly delivered meals to shut-ins with his son, had thought of himself as righteous. He had a performance-based view of God and religion and felt he was doing pretty well with his success in his job, his family, and in his church. After all of that success was stripped away, John came to realize the truth about who God was and who he was to God.

"I thought when you sin, that the Lord would be displeased with you or might reject you in some way. I didn't understand that's not the case. When you sin, you are hurting your relationship with the Lord, but he still loves you, delights in you and enjoys you. [The sin] interferes with your ability to maintain that love on your side. You're saying, 'I'm making the conscious decision to eat this crap of the side of the street instead of this porterhouse steak the Lord has for me.' I'd rather eat the steak!" laughs John who ate quite a few steaks during his ten years on Capitol Hill.

John's newfound relationship with God was, in fact, so precious to him that he risked prison rather than jeopardize it.

When the FBI show up at your door, "they don't come half-cocked," says John. They came fully armed with an arsenal of allegations and intimidation tactics designed to pressure John into cooperating. Eager to make the situation go away, John made a plea agreement to testify against a lobbyist, saying that he had taken favorable actions for the lobbyist in part because the lobbyist had given him tickets and bought him dinner (which would be illegal). As the trial dragged on, John had a personal transformation in his relationship with God, personally owned his guilt for his actions (legal or illegal), and repented for the small compromises he had been making for years.

He knew in his heart that he had acted not at all because of dinners or tickets, but completely because of the political contributions the lobbyist had made to his boss (which are legal)—an inconvenient truth for the prosecution. The details of John's actions and his plea agreement are as convoluted as the campaign finance laws which govern them (and at the printing of this book are still being appealed to the Supreme Court), but the concrete consequences of John's choice couldn't have been more clear: lie and be praised or tell the truth and risk prison.

"This is something [my kids] won't understand until they are adults at least, but when I broke the plea agreement with the government, the only people who would have known whether I was being truthful or untruthful would have been me and God. All I would have had to do was say, '[This lobbyist] gave me these tickets to [this event], and I took these actions because of that.' I could have lied. If I would have done that, I wouldn't have even gone to the halfway house. I would have been praised by the government for being their key witness. Honestly, that was tempting. But I didn't do that. I broke the plea agreement and risked going to prison for twenty-seven months. I was trusting in God and being consistent with who I was."

Maybe most people won't understand why John chose to follow his conscience over protecting his own legal self-interest. Maybe even his kids won't. The prosecution certainly didn't. But John serves a new Master now rather than the gods of Washington, D.C. He answers to a loving Father who says, "I forgive you. I love you. I have never stopped delighting in you." Would that we all had such a father. Thankfully, we do.

John served as chief of staff to Congressman Ernest Istook (R-OK). He pled guilty to honest services fraud and served four months in a halfway house for his relationship with Kevin Ring as part of the Jack Abramoff scandal. He now lives in Colorado Springs and has founded Levi's House to share with ex-convicts the good news of their identity in Christ and to help them re-enter society. John is currently writing a book about his experiences and the liberation he has found in his new understanding of God's unconditional love for him.

photo by Bryan Crump

18 MARC AND DENISE HADER—
THIRD TIME'S A CHARM: TALES OF
A SUCCESSFULLY BLENDED FAMILY

Marc and Denise Hader are in the top seven percent—not in income, but in the percentage of marriages that survive. When they married, both were single parents previously twice divorced. "The failure rate for repeat marriages is in the dumper," says Denise. With four prior failed marriages between them, they figured their marriage was ninety-three percent likely to fail.

But Denise and Marc learned from their mistakes and listened to the leading of the Holy Spirit (not statistics). They have now celebrated their statistic-breaking partnership for twelve years.

In fact, they are so happy, they had to stop leading "Divorce Care" in their church. "I was afraid we were depressing people with how happy we are," laughs Denise.

Their happiness didn't stop them from reaching out to single parents altogether, though; they still led a small group for single parents in their home, complete with child care. "Even though we weren't single anymore, we had a heart for people who had been there," says Marc. "We made sure that they could get spiritual growth and fellowship without feeling like they were abandoning their kids one more time. They tore our house up, but that's okay. We didn't mind." Denise adds, "Our girls [teenagers at the time] would watch the kids upstairs. We were downstairs, but you could sure hear them!"

Marc and Denise first met through their five-year-old daughters' gymnastic class but didn't date until several years later when Marc attended a Sunday School class with Denise's parents. "Her mom put a target on my back," laughs Marc. After spending a whole day together on Easter Sunday at her parents' house, they started dating.

A year later they married, but not without a lot of soul-searching. "We were really in love, but we were looking for reasons not to get married," says Denise. Both were cautious and didn't know if they would ever marry again. They didn't pursue a physical relationship at all. "Jumping into a physical relationship short-circuits future growth," says Marc. "Then you are focused on that. Then you are looking for reasons to make the relationship work. You don't want to upset the apple cart." Instead, they went to counseling and talked through all the tough questions first.

One of their most cherished memories is when Marc knelt down on one knee and proposed to all three of them together, Denise and their then ten-year-old daughters, Lydia and Veronica. "We wanted the girls to know that they were not an after-thought. We were going to move forward as a blended family together."

Things weren't always smooth, but they now have the joy of seeing Veronica and Lydia as independent, happily married young women (and college graduates as well). Not everyone learns from their mistakes, as the dismal success rates of second and third marriages reveal, but Denise and Marc believe that being open and honest has been crucial to their success in their marriage and in raising their girls.

"Great parents are parents who let their kids see their failure," says Denise tearfully. "Also, that God is our Savior. We fail; he forgives. Our children fail; we forgive."

The son of a preacher, Marc says he and Denise feel like they were "born on third base" into strong Christian families and had a head start toward building their own—which only made their mistakes all the more painful. "I feel like I have an advantage over most people because I have a dad who loves me beyond measure," says Denise. "So I'm able to project what my Heavenly Father looks like. Most children don't have that advantage."

Marc and Denise have been very open with their girls about their shortcomings in all areas, including sex. "The world's going to tell them, so you might as well get a headstart," says Marc. "Parents need to show that they have feet of clay." Denise adds, "I've been surprised that they haven't thrown it back in our faces. We've sat them down and been real sincere, and said, 'This is where I've blown it, don't do this.'"

Marc and Denise are honest about their shortcomings with one another as well. Marc recognized from his previous marriages that he needs help standing up for himself. He has a tendency to want to serve and to make others happy. Denise knows from her earliest relationships that she has a tendency to run over people if they let her. So they have identified the dynamic and guard against it. "I'll say, 'Hey, you're running over me!' and we'll make adjustments," laughs Marc.

They have also been honest about money and their expectation for their daughters to be independent.

"Our kids have known since they were little bitty, that we are raising them to grow up and get out," says Denise. "Of course, we say that in a loving way, but it's never been a secret. I'm always projecting out further: 'Look what you can do when you're this old! How would you get there? What would you have to do if you wanted to do this when you are older?' It's never been a secret that they are not living with us."

Marc echoes the admonition to start young, "So many parents wait until too late to start instilling values in their kids and wonder why they are terrors. They put them in all these activities or try to buy their affection instead of sitting around the table and playing board games or taking that road trip that will be a memory."

"My goal for them is to be self-sufficient," says Denise. "The Lord is first. Your spouse is second. We're raising them to start their own lives. My parents have more friends than not whose children either live with them or they support them financially in some way."

Her methods might be a little austere for some, but they worked for her girls. She practically bursts with pride at her daughters' frugalness, resourcefulness, and self-sufficiency.

When the girls were sixteen, she told Veronica and Lydia they needed to apply for five jobs or they would be grounded. "They came home that weekend with jobs at Laser Quest," Denise laughs. "Lydia had that job until she was twenty-two and got her first teaching job. If they wanted something badly enough, they could pay for it."

The same applied when it came time for college. Marc says they told the girls, "We want to be partners with you, but we can't pay for all of this. We will commit to paying for a third. We hope that you can talk your other parent into paying for a third. We want you to have some sweat equity and pay for a third as well."

Lydia chose to live at home and go to a less expensive local university. Denise laughs as she tells of how Veronica made the decision to forego her first choice of an expensive private school. After visiting the school and discovering the $32,000-a-year cost (nine years ago), Veronica said, "Did I catch that right? Did they say the best case scenario is that I would graduate and make $30,000? So I would be losing $2,000 a year? I don't want to go here." So she stayed closer to home, lived on campus, worked two jobs, and got scholarships. While Veronica's reasoning doesn't weigh all the factors involved, there's no doubt that Denise has successfully passed on her thriftiness to her daughter.

Marc, unfortunately, found himself unemployed three different times during a five-year period. "We choose to be honest with them," says Marc. "We had to say, 'We cannot help this semester.' We could have taken out loans, but we weren't going to mortgage our future." So Veronica took extra hours, got the university to frontload her scholarship money for the year, and graduated a semester early.

"She walked away with only $13,000-15,000 in student loans for a $100,000 education," beams Denise. "You have to talk about it up front. We're not afraid to talk about sex or money. And have expectations. I expected a lot of those kids."

"I'm *amazed*," she says of how the girls and their marriages have turned out. "They are truly happy. Not that they won't have problems, but it's really fabulous when they turn out the way you hoped and dreamed they would. When you're parenting, you don't know until twenty years later if it works."

19 CARLA GONZALEZ—
FOLLOWING YOUR DREAM…
(no matter how long it takes)

As Ms. America International 2012, Carla Gonzalez may now wear $6,000 gowns, jet across the country, pose in exotic photo shoots, and grace the cover of magazines, but she still remembers what it was like not to have five dollars to buy her son a toy at Wal-Mart for his class Christmas party. A small-town girl from Idabel, Oklahoma, Carla had big hopes and dreams for her life. She was enrolling in college, training for Miss Oklahoma, and dreaming of a career in fashion merchandising, acting, or modeling when those dreams came tumbling down with a positive pregnancy test at eighteen years of age.

She put aside her own dreams and chose a different path: to be a mom. She married a man who wasn't her son's biological father to give her son a family, but she still remembers the day when she decided a family at any cost wasn't worth the price.

Even twenty years later, she still struggles not to cry as she recalls the moment. She and her husband had been arguing one night when she looked outside. Her son had gone as far as he could to get away from their tension-filled house. He was standing under a streetlight, his head hung down as he stared at the ground, and all around him a light rain was falling.

That was the moment she decided he deserved better. "I still have that vision in my mind. I can't get it out. It still tears my heart out. I thought, 'He deserves better than this,'" she remembers. "You'll do for your children what you wouldn't do for yourself."

So after years of her husband's cheating and partying and emotional abuse, she decided she couldn't have her son watching and hearing it anymore. She chose to become a single parent. "It's scary to be out on your own," said Carla. "But I didn't want my son growing up doing the same things. Children learn what they live; it's environmental. I wanted him to have a better life and be a better man."

Now a clinical social worker who counsels others in similar situations, Carla believes God had a plan even for her trials. "The things I've been through have made me more patient. I can see where other people are coming from. I can tell them, 'I've been where you are.'"

Carla recognizes the significance of the mentors who helped her along the way. They encouraged her to go to school, get her degree, raise her son, and persevere through her troubled marriage.

"You need those mentors, extended family, and friends," she tells young people. "You have to have that support to be able to make it in life. If I didn't have that, I don't know." She encourages older adults to consider mentoring, "It's important for adults to take young people in. They bring different things to the table even if parents are doing a good job."

And she understood the importance of mentors in her son's life as well.

"Family cycles repeat themselves. My parents were very young when they became grandparents—thirty-six. Kyeson was the son they never had. So they stepped up to the plate and helped me raise him. My dad and he especially bonded very closely. He considers my dad, really, [his] dad. My father did everything with my son—taught him to hunt, fish, shoot a gun, everything you can think of—those 'manly' things. My uncle also totally stepped in as well, and he has two boys, too. They were all very, very close."

Determined that she and her son would not live in the poverty that so many single moms face, Carla enrolled in school at the University of Oklahoma and moved to Norman. When her dad's job took her parents to Tennessee, however, she made the difficult decision to let her son go with them, too.

"This little boy who was doing great in Idabel, was not doing well in Norman. My mom said, 'Let him come out here and stay with us until you're done with school.' So after a year, he went to live in Tennessee. I cried all the time. It was so hard. I missed him so much. As long as he was with my dad though, he was A-OK."

Despite the distance, Carla stayed active in her son's life, driving to Tennessee once a month or meeting in Idabel even though her schedule was packed with going to school full-time while working two jobs. When her dad was transferred back to Idabel, she would take annual leave every Friday so she could drive to all his high school football games all across the state. "I was such a proud mama," she says. "We have a great relationship. It's open, and we communicate well. I think it's because he always knew where he stood with me. He was number one."

Kyeson did eventually move to the city with his mom and even tried college for year, but eventually, he married and moved back to Idabel. "He's a welder and has started a hay-baling business. He makes more money than I do, and he doesn't have a degree," she laughs at the irony now that she has her masters as well as her undergraduate degree. "I'm so proud of him. He's such a good man, just a good all-round kid. He's so close with his little girl. He says, 'I will raise my children. I will set a good example for them. I'm going to have my family in church every Sunday.' He tries really hard. He sees so many kids without fathers and so many single moms raising kids alone. He says, 'I don't care [what it takes]. I'm always going to be in my kids' life.'"

And after a "twenty-year sabbatical" while raising her son, getting her degrees, counseling, teaching, and volunteering, Carla surprised everyone at age forty by picking up her own dreams of competing in the pageant world.

"I had all these dreams, and then all of a sudden, I had to make this decision: I'm going to be a mom. It was a very, very difficult time that I went through. I sucked it up and worked, worked, worked. I focused on trying to better myself and get an education, to be the best mom I could be and get him raised. But when he decided to move out and get married and do his own thing, I thought, 'What am I going to do with myself now? You know what, I'm going to get back into the pageant world just because I can.'"

So at forty years old, Carla entered her first national pageant with no coaching or prep. She entered for three years in a row. The third year, she made it to the top six. "That is because I am determined," she says. Then she entered the Miss U.S. of America pageant and got first runner-up. She went back the next year, and not only did she win, she got the highest score in every category. "That was my determination showing through again," she laughs.

Then she competed in the Ms. America pageant and got in the top twelve (Miss America contestants are seventeen to twenty-four; Ms. America contestants are twenty-six and up). She returned the next year and won her current title of Ms. America International 2012, The People's Choice, which is determined by the vote of people online all across the world. She also received fourth runner-up for Ms. America from the judges. "It was an honor because I'm competing with so many young girls," she says. "I'm in this line-up, and I'm forty-four, and the winner was twenty-seven, and two years ago she was first runner up for Miss America."

Her platforms of anti-bullying and eliminating teen dating violence fit in perfectly with the work she has done for years in schools, youth centers, and shelters educating youth about how to manage anger and eliminate violence.

From following her own dreams, she has learned you also have to let your children follow theirs.

"Being a great parent," she says, "is accepting your children for who and what they are and empowering them to find themselves and do what they want to do. My son taught me that."

For a long time, Carla would question her son's decisions about his clothes, or college, or joining a fraternity, or wearing camouflage so much.

One day, he finally confronted her, "Mom, won't you just accept me for the way that I am? You're always wanting me to do something else—things I don't want to do!"

Realizing what she'd been doing, she said, "I don't care. I love you so much. Just wear t-shirts. Be who you want to be."

"Give them appropriate guidance to grow and to flourish and become what they want to be. Because my son wants to be a farmer. I would have never picked that for him. I wanted him to be a doctor or a lawyer. But my son's so happy out there.

"He doesn't understand why I like to get all dressed up and do pageants, and I don't understand why he would want to sit out in the woods with a gun in a tree stand. But I've got to love him for who he wants to be and who he is. You have to step back and let your children grow."

20 MARY MILLER— SOWING SEEDS OF CHANGE

"The negative turns in our stories are the seeds of future trees. The only way a character can be transformed in a story is through conflict. There is no other way."

–Donald Miller, *Storyline*

Mary Miller isn't one to embrace change quickly. She still lives in the same house she bought forty years ago in Pearland, Texas, where a 170-foot white steel cross towers over the interstate, and churches with thousands of members are considered "not that big." She raised her two children, Jennifer and Donald, in a traditional Baptist culture that wasn't quick to embrace change either.

Although Mary still lives in the same house, neither she nor the church will ever be the same because of the writings and leadership of her son, Donald Miller, who challenged self-righteous, moralistic American Christian culture in his *New York Times* best-selling memoir *Blue Like Jazz: Non-Spiritual Thoughts on Christian Spirituality* which became an instant classic.

Raising two children without a father, Mary struggled to merely survive. Yet with all the audacity of her sometimes-controversial son, Mary embraced the trials, saying the best times of her life were "not the cuddly moments—it was the hard times when I knew the Lord was present."

Donald chronicles many of those hard times and pushes the boundaries of social convention in his writings. He gets that from his mom. Mary recalls one unconventional parenting moment when Donald was out playing baseball after she had asked him to put away the groceries, "I was so mad! I got in the car, went to the baseball field, and drove right up onto the field in the car." She parked the car on top of the infield next to Donald and said, "'Get. In. This. Car!' For once, he obeyed me. He got in the car. I drove home. He put the groceries away, and I drove him back to the baseball game."

Slow to change but quick to acknowledge their weaknesses, Mary says, "Donald says our family sin is pride." Yet when this proud mother is asked about her son's success she proclaims, "I don't take credit for Donald, and I don't take credit for Jennifer. It was such a struggle. I just treaded water the whole time they were growing up. The results were up to God. I never could have raised these children without God—and the church as a backdrop."

Donald and his writings have become a fresh new voice in Christianity. Between writing his best-selling books, speaking at all of his Storyline conferences, and founding The Mentoring Project, he is encouraging and equipping others "to live great stories."

Like many single parents, Mary worried whether or not her children would find success amid rebellious attitudes and struggling grades. "I defined success as being married and having 2.3 children and a good job, just like everybody else does. Well, that's not how Donald came into success, and he is still not defining it that way." Mary was recently reminded how far they have both come when Donald called home asking Mary for his shot records. She called the high school, and they sent his whole transcript. "He was 244th out of like 360 people. I'm trying to say, he was close to the bottom of his class in grades. But at the time, all I could see was grades. And I was thinking, 'What kind of future is this kid gonna have?'"

To become a better mother Mary not only had to change herself, but her definition of success which "was very difficult." Donald is helping others to do the same in his conferences and new book *Storyline: Finding your Subplot in God's Story.*

Ironically, Mary felt she was sacrificing for her kids by attending the church that Donald so famously criticizes. "I chose the church for them. I wouldn't have chosen it for myself." Mary realized early on that "you have to find community outside of your home. And church is a good place to go. We didn't have a lot of money, so church was our social life."

If she had it to do over again, "I would've talked more. I would've asked them how they felt more. I would have criticized less. I had no idea how much not having a father affected them. We never talked about it." Still she does not regret choosing the church that would transform the way all of them would view Christianity and organized religion, and ultimately change these viewpoints for others around the world.

"Donald found David Gentiles there," his youth pastor who encouraged him to write and the man to whom he dedicated *Blue Like Jazz.* "I did some things right. They were raised in church. I asked men [at church] to teach him how to work, how to read the Bible, and how to interact with men. That's all you can do is plant those seeds."

Now Donald is the one planting seeds. "He has changed me. He has shown me how to show grace. I learn a lot from him. He's maturing. He's studying more. He's studying the Bible." Mary also approves of the relationships he intentionally cultivates with other leaders, "He gets that from me. Come beside someone who's better than you, someone who has accomplished things, someone wiser than you and learn from them."

Mary believes we are never too old to learn new things. She went back to school for her MBA at fifty after her children left home. She had her guestroom professionally decorated to host weary travelers and serves tea and cookies to a small group of young women whom she mentors every Wednesday night. She credits Donald and his writings for the switch. He's planting seeds of change, not only in the church, but in his own family.

Yet change took time. At first Mary reacted like many of Donald's critics asking, "What's wrong with fundamentalism? What's wrong with tradition?

What's wrong with dressing up when you go to church and not having loud music? You know, leave it alone," Mary chuckles. After reading *Blue Like Jazz*, Mary says, "I was not comfortable. I thought, what am I gonna tell this kid?" So Mary told him, "You are an amazing writer. But it's not gonna fly well in my zip code. I have to live with these people, Donald!" Mary has a great sense of humor about it now, but it wasn't always so easy. "He was criticizing my church, the church he grew up in!"

The Miller family embraces each other's differences the same way they have learned to embrace change, as integral to their personal and spiritual growth. "He's ruined me!" Mary laughs as she relents, "I can't be happy with singing all five stanzas of a hymn, and I'm not quite happy with the band up there either!" At age sixty-eight she recently transferred her church membership to a new church plant that is reaching out to the un-churched in downtown Houston saying, "He's changed me. I'm somewhere in the middle. I was so comfortable [at my old church], but I did not want to be comfortable. I don't want that anymore."

21 WINGSPAN ESSAY WINNERS— IN THEIR OWN WORDS

The following four essays were chosen as the top stories from single parents in the Wingspan inspiring essay contest:

Regina Brandt—Rising Above Autism

When my little girl was born, I knew something wasn't quite right. She rejected everyone, even her poor father. If anyone else attempted to hold her or even just coo to her, Sierra would scream until either I was able to soothe her or she passed out hours later soaked with sweat from exhaustion. Our beautiful blue-eyed baby girl couldn't seem to connect with anyone else but me. Over time it wore her father down and that combined with other marital problems— well, it eventually became just the two of us.

It took a long time to get a diagnosis. Either ill-informed people insisted she was just fine, or those that knew what was wrong didn't want to 'label' my tiny little girl. All I could think to say was, "If she had leukemia, wouldn't you want to label her so that she could get treatment?" She was three and a half when I finally heard the word *autism*. Her father and I were individually told, "Even the best parents need to know when to give up and put their kid in a home on medication." I cried about it; I prayed about it. And in the end, I dried my eyes and told God, "I'm going to bust my a** for a miracle, and you're going to give it to me." With refreshed resolve, I fired everyone that agreed with giving up and found people with even a glimmer of optimism that things could be better for Sierra. From that day on, I never let anyone decide for Sierra what her best outcome was going to be: I knew we were still working towards her best possible future.

Everyone seemed to have lots of different ideas about what results we could expect interventions to produce. Each time we met an expert's highest expectations for Sierra's recovery we would, with grateful hearts, move on to the next therapist who had more hope to offer Sierra. With all of the experts we saw, no one seemed to have a clear vision of where we were going with all of these different interventions. Each therapist did their own thing quietly and competently, but there was no leadership. I realized that I was the captain of this ship—and this boat was sinking fast!

I screwed up my courage and took charge. It was intimidating to tell people with degrees and half the alphabet behind their names what the plan was; but even so, I chose three goals at a time from Sierra's ABA [Applied Behavioral Analysis] Therapy book. I would write my golden-haired girl's three goals down and share them with everyone we came in contact with, from speech therapists to grocery store clerks. Each person was surprisingly receptive to participating in our exercises and the other therapists incorporated our three weekly homework goals into their treatments. It got to the point that even our favorite cashier would ask, "What are today's goals?" eager to be part of our blossoming miracle. Each person who touched us and helped Sierra learn to make eye contact became a chance for Sierra to connect, to function, to take another tiny step towards being more fully human instead of a distant angel lost in the mist. Defeating autism was to quote *A Bug's Life,* was "an epic adventure in miniature proportions." All of Sierra's gains were so small but came with great effort.

I figured out that autism must hurt a lot because when I treated my screaming angel for pain, it brought us both peace. Her tone little body would relax, the screaming eventually tapered off, and we were able to soldier on another day. Knowing Sierra hurt, I understood that I had to make her therapy fun. I asked myself, "What would it take to get me out of bed if I had the flu complete with body aches?" It would have to be something awesome! So, I made Sierra's childhood as wonderful as I could. As grueling as autism was for me, Sierra's days were fun-filled and rewarding.

Sierra and I worked hard and played endlessly while doing her ABA Therapy, eventually increasing her visits to twice a week to keep up with her rapid advances. I literally narrated every aspect of her life in a sing-song voice so that she would hear the words that went with the activity. I changed her diet to wheat and dairy-free, so that the proteins wouldn't pollute her system and contribute to the fog that kept her locked away inside herself. Well, the results were awesome! The glassy haze left her eyes and instead of being completely silent, Sierra began to respond to my questions with one- to three-word sentences! And finally, but most importantly, I would celebrate Sierra's smallest achievements with the equivalent of a New York City ticker tape parade.

Autism was hard. I tell you as a battered and starved child myself, that having an child in the grips of autism was the worst thing that ever happened to me. Autism doesn't just affect the one family member. Autism takes hostages. You can't leave your child unattended for even a second to go potty—they disappear, slipping outside or quietly into a cabinet. When they aren't screaming, they are dead silent. They don't even respond to their own names, so you can imagine the panic you feel while looking for them after an urgent and long-delayed trip to the loo [bathroom]. You can't take a shrieking thrashing child into the grocery store, and you can't predict when a meltdown is going to occur, or even how long it is going to last; so restaurants, haircuts, and basically any ordinary mommy-and-me outing is out. The worst part is the glares from strangers and the mean comments telling you to hit your kid for behavior they have no control over. One parent summed it up best, "Everyone just stares at you making these ugly comments, and you have this kicking screaming thrashing kid writhing to get out of your hands, and you obviously need help, but no one will help you. They won't even hold the door so you can leave." It happened to me a few times, too, though I harbor no anger; they simply failed a test of compassion.

Every time I hit a wall, prayer was my only and truly best alternative. Either I was thanking God for our recent advances and various blessing, or I would literally tell God I was empty and exhausted and I needed Him to intervene. Sometimes I didn't even know what we needed next, but (usually in tears) I gave Him my heart's desire. And our prayers would be answered, often in a handful of days. Even through all of the challenges and rejections, there were the constant answers to my prayers and fine examples of human kindness. We found a great and compassionate pediatrician on our first try. A new dental clinic with an awesome dentist who had a heart for struggling children opened just at the time we needed them. Strangers would often approach me and offer kind words of encouragement. One store clerk who knew us offered up loudly on an especially rough trip to the store, "Oh, honey! Are you having a bad autism day? Don't worry, I'll get to you right quick!" creating the opportunity for formerly glowering patrons to offer us a place near the front of the line. All of the pain and hardship was laced with unexpected kindness and imbued with God's continuing presence. That's what makes our family so special: witnessing firsthand how much God will give you if you just ask and how close God will hold you in the darkest of places.

I read somewhere that being a single mother is almost a guarantee for poverty. Even so, we lead a rich life full of wonder and joy. Sierra is thirteen now and all but recovered from autism. She smiles when she tells me that she had the best childhood! If you met her today, you'd be impressed by her gracious manners, playful/impish nature and her sweet, articulate (albeit short) conversations. You would never guess she had been coaxed back into this world like mist through a key hole. Sometimes my friends will point out that I worked really hard for this recovery. That is true, but I am in awe of Sierra because, as hard as I worked for her recovery, Sierra had to earn the results, and she sure does shine! I am in awe of my daughter's accomplishments and grateful to our God for giving her back to me. I can't wait to see what's in store for us next!

Crystal Schultz—Beauty from Ashes

"Sometimes He calms the storm; sometimes He calms the sailor. Sometimes He holds the whole torrential terror in His hands." – Unknown

My family consists of a precious little boy—doe-eyed, olive skin with a darling dimple on his right upper-cheek who loves building, reading, snuggling—oh yeah, and myself.

April 18, 2008, the day after my son was born, he and I had a very sweet moment together during the quiet hours of the morning. The nurse brought a swaddled bundle with a pacifier nearly bigger than his head. I held him nose-to-nose with me and whispered, "No matter what the future holds, Mama and Mason will always be together."

My sweet Mason is four years old now, but our journey began almost two years ago. Our path has been rocky; the enemy of all good things has thwarted it. But, by God's grace and blind faith, Mason and I have been given the chance to make this a beautiful story of resilience.

I was driving through my little, cozy suburb one January day with my toddler singing in the backseat when my phone rang. My husband. He'd had a bad day. I consider myself a realist mostly, but also often the glass-half-full type. So when my husband told me that the police wanted to question him regarding a teenage girl's accusation, but that it was a total mistake—a prank gone bad, if you will—my immediate thought was that a good attorney could squash any false account. I drove to my three-bedroom, two-bathroom, decorated and heated home to my husband and dog. We were the picture of a happy family living in the suburbs. "Everything is fine, and we'll get past this without a hitch," I thought to myself. "I mean, the accusations aren't true, right?"

It was only twenty-four short hours later that I was in my pastor's office, also known as my dad's work office. In utter confusion, crying and yelling, I recounted my husband's hour-old confession to my father. What did people do in this situation? When their spouse had not only betrayed them, but also broken the law, in one single act? Obviously, my dad was confused and also feeling extremely hurt by this man who had taken his only daughter for marriage and then stained it.

"Pack some things for yourself and Mason and get over to our house. Assure him that you haven't made any permanent decisions, that you just need a vacation from your house for a few days while you sort this out in your head." I did exactly what my dad told me to do. I was in no shape to make any decision for myself at the moment. "What had I done wrong?" This wasn't the first time I'd felt betrayed by my husband, but by far the only act that involved someone else.

When I finally felt the strength to recount my decisions and thoughts, I journaled this: "The coldest winter I remember in so, so many ways."

I remember the moment perfectly. I was in shambles. My stomach had been sick for days. I couldn't eat. I slept quite a bit. I worried most every moment that I was awake. Oh, and I had a toddler. It was freezing outside. I was desperately grasping for answers, but it was too incredibly foggy. I couldn't see a bit of clarity outside of my parenting duties and my love for Mason.

I was so fed up. I couldn't handle the addiction any longer. Not only did it hurt like hell, it was tearing everything I held dear apart. Everything except one thing: being his mom.

My family was broken. My work slipped.

God gave me so much grace and empowered me to be a mommy despite it all. It seems that Mason has always been a part of the tangible grace God granted me.

I stood in the shower with my hands in the air, then on the wall, hysterical. Not my shining moment. I told God that I was weary from this journey. I was lonely and afflicted. I told Him that I knew he had given me choices regarding my marriage, in this situation. Then I told Him that I had made my decision. I was going. I told God I couldn't imagine living this life any longer, not knowing if the addiction would go away or not. Selfishly, I wanted it to go away for me. Or, at the very least, for Mason. But I knew, deep down, that wasn't how this monster worked. It had to be gone for other reasons. There had to be a yearning for a divine intervention, and I seemed to be the only one asking for it.

When I presented my decision to God, He told me something. I remember it so well. It was not quite audible, but I felt it. I was on my knees, water pouring on my back, with my hands trying to brace myself from putting my head through a bathroom wall, begging for His blessing on this awful thing… "I will never leave you, nor forsake you. Now rest."

Mason's dad had hit rock bottom and saw him one or two times each week for the first few months, but where he wasn't and couldn't be in Mason's life, my father and brothers stepped in beautifully. We went through potty training, a change in preschools and homes, and a transition for me at work going from part-time to full-time during this time period. With all of the support that my family and two close friends provided, Mason seemed minimally affected.

By April, I had already been a single parent for more than three months, and it was time to protect my son and myself legally. A very hurtful nine months later, my divorce was final. The judge ruled that my now ex-husband's actions didn't pertain to his ability to parent, so with joint custody we moved forward.

I have only God to praise and thank for the wake-up call he gave my son's father. Mason is happy, loved, cared-for, and adjusting beautifully. I cannot judge Mason's father's personal growth, but I do know that he loves his son, and I am forever glad for that.

Out of prayers answered and the light at the end of the tunnel in sight, I journaled this around the time our court case began:

"..But this happened so that the works of God might be displayed in him."—John 9:3

All of John 9 is about a blind man's healing. Everyone thought that the man had done something to deserve his blindness. Isn't that completely silly? Hello, no one chooses these things. Who wants to be ridiculed, betrayed, hurt, handicapped, and scarred for life?

Mason was born with two birthmarks and his mama's teeth (bless him). Poor little guy didn't ask for these things and absolutely did nothing to receive them... And, someday, Mason may feel a little self conscious because of his flaws. If and when he does (ahem, adolescence), I may just have the opportunity to tell him for the millionth time how I think he is absolutely, without a flinch, the most handsome child ever birthed on this planet. His physical "flaws" are not flaws at all to his mama; they are beautiful reminders that he is mine.

If I could photograph my world right now, it would be full of things I didn't choose. Someone else (Satan...if we're being specific) birthed these things, and now I have to live with them. I'm only allowed to choose my reaction. I'd really like to beat a flipping punching bag to shreds some days and just let everyone within seventy-five miles know how much it hurts.

I don't know what the blind man's life looked like outside of the miracle moment—he may have punched a camel to death—but I do know that he let God's glory shine through his healing and that is what someone remembered to write down.

Profoundly to have God's work on display in my life—that is what I want. And the scars? They will be beautiful reminders that I am His.

La Shell Winston—Never Give Up

La Shell Winston's road to single parenting was paved with death, murder, and abuse, yet through hard work, perseverance, and faith her future is bright. Despite all odds she has pursued her lifelong goal to be a nurse, teaching her three boys "not to look at the negative—that everything happens for a reason." Their motto is, "It happened for a reason," but her story teaches us to "never give up."

From an early age, La Shell was no stranger to divorce. "When I was ten, I was with my father on one of his planned visitation days, and I was visiting some of his family that lived in Spencer, Oklahoma. My Dad and I went to the store." While her Dad went in, she recalls, "These men started shooting. They had been driving around, drinking, opened their glove box, and [saw] a 22." A stray bullet went through the trailer, grazing her hand and piercing her neck.

La Shell turned tragedy into triumph. "All through school I knew I wanted to be a nurse because of the time I spent in the hospital recovering. It was a nurse who helped me to learn how to write again, talk again, and be able to move my neck from side to side. So I attended Mid-Del Vo-Tech in the practical nursing program, and I did well."

After nursing school La Shell went to Langston University where she "met her soul mate and moved to Kansas City, Missouri. The fourth year I was there I got pregnant with my son Richard." One night "my son's father didn't come home from 'work.' I called his family looking for him, and no one had seen him. One of my co-workers at the hospital called me the next morning and told me that she thought that [he] was there and told me to come up. When I got to my job, I was met by two police officers, three investigators, and a doctor. I was five months pregnant at the time." She expected them to take her to a hospital room, but instead, unbeknownst to her, they were headed toward the morgue area.

As they walked, one of the officers said, "Shell, [are] you going to be alright?"

She burst into tears realizing she would never see the father of her child again. Despite the doctor's warning that the body was unidentifiable, La

Shell insisted on seeing for herself.

"When they opened the drawer where he was, all I [could] see was like something off the movies. It was a body that was burnt to almost nothing. I felt numb." Then she fainted.

When she woke up in a hospital bed, investigators began to tell her about her fiancé and his family's lifestyle, and she realized that she was part of one of Kansas's largest drug families. Advised that it would be best for her and her unborn child to leave the state, she moved to Oklahoma to begin a new life.

Continuing to pursue her dream to work in health care, she got a job at a major hospital in Oklahoma City. Almost six years later, "I ran across an old classmate who came into my life and changed my world." The happy couple conceived her second child, Jeremiah, but tragedy struck again. "As I am having Jeremiah, his father was picked up by the FBI. They were looking for him in Atlanta for killing a police officer. So again, I was left sad, shocked, and confused. I fell for another man God hadn't chosen for me."

"I packed up and moved. I kept my focus on school and continued my education by doing online courses. I soon became office manager of this new behavioral health unit, and I loved it!" La Shell began dating during this time and she got pregnant again.

But after three years, "things started to go sour. Out of all of my break-ups this was the most violent. As we started to move in different directions he broke into my house and stole all of my stuff. He came to my job and busted all of the windows out of my car along with stealing the car. He jumped me one night [when] I was leaving work and put me in the hospital for three days. Again, God didn't choose him, I did."

La Shell's grandmother encouraged her to read the Bible where she discovered "I was like Nicodemus. He was all wild, and then he was like, 'Okay God, what do I have to do to serve you?'" On dating now she says, "I'm very leery. I'm going to let God choose [the next] one."

God may not have chosen those men, but he chose to gift La Shell with "the best kids in the world." Her three boys, Richard, Jeremiah, and Melvin have given La Shell the strength to overcome. "If I didn't have my kids, I wouldn't be this strong. I've got boys, how can you give up?" In addition to the normal burdens of a single parent, La Shell also struggles with her sons' disabilities. Although eighteen, Richard is developmentally delayed with the mental capabilities of a nine- or ten-year-old. Jeremiah (age twelve) suffers from bi-polar and explosive anger disorder and Melvin Jr. (age six) has ADHD. Even with all of the challenges that come with their special needs, her boys have maintained "a heart of gold and a spirit that puts you at ease."

Motivated to teach her boys to battle continually against the challenges set before them, La Shell found the inspiration to enroll in Southern Nazarene University telling them, "Mama's in her forties, and she's still in school." She earned her bachelors in organizational leadership. On the day of graduation a friend from school, Karen Bub, invited her to attend the Single Parent Support Network's 'Queen for a Day' event. Because La Shell was resistant due to numerous other obligations, Karen had to be persistent. "The day I was to walk across the stage to get my certificate for my bachelors is the day I was told I needed to attend the conference. And that was the day I got the grant from Kevin Durant!"

La Shell won $2,000 that day thanks to the Single Support Network's Kevin Durant Grant and a faithful friend who had submitted her story to the organization before the event. The money came at a critical time in her life. "As the holidays started coming I realized that I was so focused on bills, my kids had nothing for Christmas. And I was about to graduate. I had an electric bill that was due, and it was about $1,000." Unable to survive without electricity, due to a medical condition which required her to breathe through a machine each night, La Shell saw the grant as an answer to her prayers.

God didn't stop there. "I came back to work the next day telling everyone, 'Oh my gosh, I'm so thankful. Now I can pay my electric bill. And Karen (the same co-worker who brought her to the Single Parent Support Network) was like, 'My church paid your electric bill.'" La Shell tried to pay her back with the grant money, "But she said, 'Nuh uh, that money is for you and your boys.'" The blessings just kept coming.

"My boss invited me and the kids over on Christmas Eve to her house. We went over there, and one of the other ladies we work with said, 'We're gonna go over and clean your house because we know you can't do too much.' When me and my kids came home, we had all of these Christmas presents under the tree that the two clinics gave to me and my kids. I was like, 'Oh my gosh, are you serious?!' I can't believe they did that for me. It was awesome. I was so humbled."

Currently, La Shell is working on her masters in health care while raising her three boys, all of whom are struggling with disabilities. Yet she says "I've just been blessed a lot. My words to single parents are that you can make it no matter what. Now I look back at everything and think, 'Wow, I survived that.'"

Traci Ann Scott—Grand Prize Winner

Life, for me, has always been a struggle. It seemed I was always battling illness—a constant feeling of nausea, being tired, migraine headaches and an endless struggle with weight. At age twenty-five, I was finally diagnosed with type one diabetes. Then three years later I was diagnosed with poly-cystic ovary syndrome. I was told I would probably not have any more children. But God was determined I would. With six pregnancies, I was blessed with three beautiful, healthy, thriving children.

For a while, life was really good. Kids were growing and starting school. Aside from taking small, short-term jobs, I was blessed to be a stay-at-home mom. My husband, Jake, had a secure government job. We felt so thankful and blessed during this time. Then one day he became severely ill. His blood sugar suddenly spiked to over 1,000. He was running a fever of 105 and was out of his mind. He ended up in ICU and spent several weeks in the hospital. Once he was released, it was another four months before he returned to work. He made a full physical recovery, but financially, it was too much for us. Soon the bank took our home, and we sold nearly all the contents inside it. This was a loss he never got over.

In September of 2009, laying on the couch feeling sorry for myself, incredibly unhappy and more than 100 pounds overweight, I heard the audible voice of God: "Get up and do something about it!" At the time, I was working and suffering further health problems. I, with Jake's full support, quit my job and decided I would focus fully on my health. By March of 2010, I was well on my way. I had lost fifty pounds and was feeling really good. All the areas of our life had seemed to fall into proper place, and it was good! After nearly ten years, we were going to be able to buy our own home—no more renting, no more shame of living with his mother. We both had big hopes and dreams. This time we were going to make them happen.

I could see the excitement in his eyes the second we pulled into the driveway. This felt like the "one." By description, it had everything we were looking for. We decided to hop out of the car and see if the back gate was open. It was! We turned the corner of the house to find a bi-level patio. It was perfect. The kids would love the pool, and there was not much yard to mow. We started making plans on flowers and yard furniture and a fire pit. Oh, and a swing in the shade over by the storage building. Then the realtor popped her head around the corner to let us know she had arrived. Finally, we could see the inside! It was everything we had been dreaming of. It was home—a very large living room with a ceiling that was a mile high, hard wood floors, freshly painted walls, built-in bookcase, master bedroom downstairs, office/den space, a huge kitchen with an eat-in dining area, and a room for everyone. We were already picking out the kids rooms and where to place furniture. The kitchen would be a great place for us to all hang out and have fun. This was it!

After a while of wrestling and praying with the decision to purchase the home, we decided we were going to make an offer. We didn't get the chance. Two days later he passed on. It was devastating. Our whole world fell to pieces. I was left here with three kids with no home. I didn't have a job, much less any experience to get one that would support the four of us. But in the moment that I discovered his lifeless body, I felt the presence of the Holy Spirit there with me. Although my heart was broken and my world shattered, I have had a peace inside that is unexplainable.

I realize now that God had a purpose for me to "Get up and do something about it!" I was blessed with the opportunity to spend a lot of time with the love of my life and was able to focus on my health. I lost a total of 110 pounds making me healthier and strong enough to care for my children and live a long, happy life.

Today, my three beautiful children and I live in the home that Jake picked for us. I have often times felt his presence here with us. I laugh as if he had had an argument with God about checking in on us and had won. God has blessed me with the opportunity to return to school. I recently received my associates degree and am currently working towards my bachelors degree. I have also had the awesome opportunity to watch Madison, Alyson, and Dawson handle themselves with such dignity and grace. They are truly children of God. Life for us has certainly not been easy. We still have our struggles, just like every family, but all my hope, faith, trust, my everything, I have put in God. He has been so faithful to provide all our needs and more.

22 SHERIFF JOHN WHETSEL–
REDEEMING HORRIFIC LOSS

Oklahoma County Sheriff John Whetsel can still recount every detail of the day he became a single parent more than thirty years ago. The chief of the Choctaw Police at the time, Whetsel had left for work early knowing he would be staying late for a board meeting. His wife, Darlene, had taken their two daughters, Stacy (four) and Rebecca (two), to her parents' house so they could swim and have dinner since he would be coming home late.

He had stopped at a fireworks stand on his way home to get ready for the family's Fourth of July celebration when he heard over his radio the information about a high-speed chase that had ended in a collision.

Above: A cherished photo of Sherriff Whetsel and his daughter Stacy in the play room of the hospital following the accident which claimed the lives of his wife and daughter

Three motorcyclists had been street racing nearby, and an officer had gone in pursuit. Two of the cyclists pulled over and surrendered, but the police officer continued to pursue the third motorcyclist who had turned into a residential neighborhood where the speed limit was twenty-five miles per hour.

"The chase was being conducted at 100 miles per hour," says Sheriff Whetsel. "The police cruiser was out-driving its lights and sirens." The cruiser followed the cyclist through a stop sign crashing into a compact car broadside at 100 mph.

Responding to the request for assistance, he approached the scene of twisted metal and flashing lights. Even in the darkness he could see the crushed police cruiser and the small compact car it had literally split in two upon impact. He recalls, "An ambulance had already arrived. I saw the law enforcement officer being loaded in the ambulance. I went to check to see how he was doing and assure him everything was going to be okay."

Within ten to fifteen minutes, the ambulance driver came over with the body of a child wrapped in a sheet and laid it on the floor of the ambulance at Whetsel's feet asking if he would watch over the body.

"I remember a bright light coming on from the wrecker, and it lit up the car. I saw an 'Andy Coates for U.S. Senate' bumper sticker on the car. And I saw a [police] badge [on the license plate]. Then I looked under the car [which was split in half] as it was being lifted [off her body], and I saw the shirt of the lady who was underneath the car, and for the first time, I realized it was my family's car."

"Then I realized that the body laying next to me had to be the body of one of my children."

Words can't convey the grief that came with that realization. Whetsel ran out of the ambulance toward the car and was restrained by other officers "who couldn't believe it was my family." They led him to a patrol car and were trying to comfort him when a medical professional on the scene approached.

"Do you have a daughter named Stacy?" she asked.

"Yes," he answered.

"She needs you," she said.

Those three words gave Sheriff Whetsel hope, "For the first time, I knew that one of my children had survived."

He would learn later that his four-year-old daughter Stacy had actually been in the back seat of the car. When the car caught on fire upon impact, a man had heard her screams and broken out the back window of the car in order to pull her out and save her life.

They loaded Stacy in an ambulance and went to Midwest City Hospital. "At the hospital, they told me what I already knew: that my wife and two-year-old daughter were dead. Stacy and I became the two survivors of our family."

What he didn't know then was that Stacy was not expected to survive. They were only trying to stabilize her so they could send her to Children's Hospital. By the time they arrived, word had gotten out among law enforcement officers about the crash. He remembers vividly walking between a line of officers from the back of the ambulance into the emergency room door. "You always hear about 'the blue line,'" says Sheriff Whetsel obviously still touched by the display. "I thought that was a tremendous showing of support from law enforcement."

At the hospital, they performed exploratory surgery to remove her spleen and repair other internal injuries, but Stacy didn't get better—she got worse. "I don't remember a whole lot about that week," says John. "I was almost physically removed from the hospital so that we could make funeral arrangements. I remember picking out matching caskets for my wife and two-year-old, picking out funeral plots—things I shouldn't have had to be doing at age thirty."

The only time he would leave the hospital would be at night after Stacy was asleep, and then he would go to the funeral home. "I would spend hours at the funeral home with the caskets," he remembers. "I never did get to see their bodies."

Stacy wasn't well enough to attend the funeral, but she had such a remarkable recovery within the next twenty-four hours that she was allowed to walk out of the hospital with her dad the next day.

"Stacy and I began rebuilding our lives." They took a three-week driving trip together through Colorado, Arizona, and Utah, driving at night and going to amusement parks during the day. "I would try to drive at night while she slept. I wanted to spend the time she was awake doing fun stuff."

"But when we got home, the pain was still there. The loss was still there. I realized that trying to take a trip to ease the pain didn't work, but it did give us three great weeks together. It had never just been the two of us before. I didn't have any instructions on how to make that work."

"There was a point and time that I became really bitter," admits Sheriff Whetsel. "The fact that the officer never apologized didn't help either." The law enforcement officer involved in the crash was charged with negligent homicide, but the trial resulted in a hung jury. The trial was so difficult for Sheriff Whetsel that he told the district attorney that he didn't want to go through another trial. "I wanted retribution, but it always came back to— I'm the only one that's there for my daughter, so if I did something stupid, she never would have anybody else."

The pain was so great that it was ten years before he could talk about the crash, but he talks about it now because he knows his story can save lives.

"I've always wanted to make sure that the deaths of Darlene and Rebecca were not in vain, that they had some meaning. I've tried to give that meaning through traffic safety programs throughout the world. I share this story with law enforcement officers, difficult as it is, because it gets their attention that traffic safety can save lives, one stop at a time."

"I know the crash has had a direct impact on the way law enforcement does business, not only in the state of Oklahoma, but around the world," says Sheriff Whetsel. Within six months of the crash, new guidelines and driver training programs were established for law enforcement officers in the state of Oklahoma for the first time, and those guidelines have spread to a national level. He says of his wife of the last eighteen years, Mitzi, "She knows I have a mission. Once a month or so, I'm invited by some law enforcement group around the country to give my presentation. Having that support from my wife has been fantastic."

His work in traffic safety has brought healing, too, but his real strength comes from his faith. "I was raised in a Christian home. I believe God has a plan and purpose for everything. It was really difficult to let [my wife and daughter] go, but even at the funeral, we did so with the knowledge and hope that we would see them again. I think that was helpful to me, the Christian belief that life has just changed its form from being with us to being in heaven."

"One of the things I still don't understand, however, is why the crash happened. But one of these days, I'll get the answer," he says with both a smile and a tear in his eye. "One of these days I'll ask that question at the appropriate time."

Sheriff John Whetsel has served in law enforcement for over forty years and as Oklahoma County Sheriff for more than sixteen. He is a nationally-recognized authority on traffic safety and police pursuits, receiving numerous awards, and has appeared on the *Phil Donahue Show*, *Larry King Live*, *Dateline*, *NBC Nightly News*, *Hard Copy*, *Front Page*, *America's Most Wanted* and *You be the Judge*. In addition, he has testified before Congressional committees and legislative hearings as part of his aggressive campaign to save lives through better training, awareness, and standards.

The Whetsel family now includes his wife Mitzi, daughters Jonna Whetsel and Stacy Moore, son-in-law Brock and grandchildren Bailey, Kailey, and Caitlin. Sheriff Whetsel talks with his family often and closes every conversation by telling them he loves them. He says, "You never know when you might not get another chance to say that to them."

photo by Bryan Crump

23 SONJA JOHNS–
THE THERAPIST ASKS FOR HELP

"I turned on the lamp, and he was gray," remembers Sonja Johns, therapist, wife, and mother of two. Just one week before, her husband Chris was fine.

Sonja remembers him as being "very down to earth and simple, just an easy-going guy who never got his feathers ruffled and married this very feisty girl who always got her feathers ruffled!" Chris was perfect for Sonja.

"He just enjoyed life. He didn't need a lot to keep himself happy. He didn't need fancy things, and he really and truly just liked being home with his family. He and our son, Jackson, were little buddies. [Chris] could always find a way for Jackson to help. If he was running a saw in the garage, he would give Jackson a broom to sweep up the sawdust underneath. He always had a way for Jackson to be involved. The two of them would just disappear on Saturdays, and I wouldn't see them for hours. They would have been to all kinds of places and just done stuff."

Chris was not only a great father, but a great friend, too. "He was very helpful. If someone needed help moving, building, fixing, or whatever—Chris was there." Chris spent his life helping others, but as a fatal blood clot began developing in his brain, there was no one who could help him.

Chris's health declined rapidly. After not feeling well for a couple of days, he went to the doctor who told him he looked fine. Chris was a young and healthy thirty-four-year-old. The doctor assumed he was probably just dehydrated and worn out. "So Chris came home. He had a meeting at church that evening, and I had a work meeting. We let Jackson (who was three at the time) stay the night with my in-laws, which we never did during the week—sometimes on the weekend, but never during the week. But because it was going to be late when we got home, we let him stay over there."

Chris called Sonja from home and said, "I'm running a fever. Do you think that's a problem?"

"Why don't you call the emergency number just to be sure?" Sonja suggested.

Once again the doctor reassured Chris that he was fine.

When Sonya got home from the meeting a little after ten, Chris was lying on the couch resting and said he was feeling better. Little did they know that was the last night Sonja would ever spend with her husband.

"I think it probably was just a virus. I took some Tylenol, and it passed," Chris lovingly reassured her.

"So we talked that night," recalls Sonja. "We sat on the couch and talked for hours. We talked about everything." What made their relationship special was that "Chris was not just my husband, he was my best friend."

"We went to bed well after midnight. He had been feeling short of breath and just real run down, but he said, 'I think I feel better.' So we went to sleep. I remember hearing him get up in the night to go to the bathroom. I woke up, and he was making this horrible choking, gasping noise. I thought he was snoring, so I nudged him, and it didn't stop." In the darkness Sonja called out, "Are you okay?" And he didn't even respond. "I turned on the lamp, and he was gray and sweating. I knew something was wrong, so I pulled him up. I thought, 'If I can get him sitting up, he'll be better. So I pulled him up and got him to the edge of the bed and he kept saying, 'I'm okay. I'm okay. I'm okay.' But he never really opened his eyes and talked to me. He could tell me that he couldn't breathe, and his chest didn't hurt. I thought he was having a heart attack. I called 911, and the paramedics came in, and the firemen came in. Thankfully, Jackson was at his grandparents; he wasn't home. By the time they got the leads on him and started the machine, it was like 'beep beep beep, beeeeeeeeeep.'"

The paramedics and doctors worked on John for hours from the gurney to the hospital. Sonja waited patiently in a waiting room until the doctor came in and said, "There's nothing we can do, he didn't make it." "I told him, 'Well, but I'm pregnant,' like, since you know that, you can do something else," she says, now laughing at the ridiculousness of her statement. Chris had died due to a massive blood clot.

Even in those darkest moments, Sonja was always thinking of others. "In the E.R., I don't remember crying. I remember having to comfort different people," she chuckles. "But that's just kind of how I am. I'll keep going, and I'll deal with myself later."

"I was pregnant," with gestational diabetes. "I had to eat, and I had to sleep for the baby. Jackson was three. Three-year-olds don't cease to exist. They still get up in the mornings and..." her sentence trails as she smiles knowingly, her eyes dancing along another kind of trail left behind by her youngest in the living room. "So my response was that I have to be healthy for this baby and for my three-year-old. I had no choice; it just was."

A few months before her daughter Katie was born, Sonja's doctor asked, "How are you doing?"

She responded, "You know, I'm just really starting to feel like I can't do this. Everything is a big deal."

As an occupational therapist, Sonja's job is to allow people to lean on her for help until they have the strength and ability to operate on their own. Yet when life became crippling, she found herself unable to lean on others.

Her doctor continued to ask Sonja about counseling, but she resisted saying, "No. I'm a therapist. I'm an occupational therapist. I just know routine is good. That's what you do."

The doctor finally persuaded Sonja that she wouldn't have to see a counselor for a long time but insisted that she needed to see somebody. At her first appointment Sonja told her counselor, "Listen, I'm not big on laying on the couch and telling people my problems. I'm not gonna look at your ink spots. I'm not doing this. I want you to set some real goals. I want you to tell me how long we're gonna work on them, and I'll do them. And then I'm out of here in a month or two."

Nobody wants to see a therapist less than a therapist. "We're not supposed to be the ones who need help. We are helpers. We are fixers. It's hard for somebody like that to say, 'I need help,' and maybe, to admit that you need some help. I can't fix myself? Seriously? Let's be honest, it's a crazy huge thing. Nobody would ever think anything about someone who lost their husband and has two babies [going to counseling], but I thought, 'No! I'm not going to be dependent on a counselor.' And do I feel like my patients are co-dependent because they depend on me? No way. They need me. But I wasn't going to need anybody." Once again laughing at herself Sonja quips, "Well, four years and some months later, I'm still with her."

"I've always been stubborn. If something bothers you, you fix it." Yet when it comes to therapy Sonja found that "it's a safe place to go and unload all the stuff that builds up. You don't have to bother anyone else about it. I went through a time when people would do the head tilt and give a sympathetic look and ask 'How are you?' But they didn't really want to know."

"My friends at church, my in-laws, my sister, my parents, they all lost someone too. I lost my best friend, my husband, my kids' dad. But Kay lost her son, Stacy lost her brother-in-law, my mom lost her son-in-law. [He filled] a role for them. We were really close to several couples, and they lost their friend. So for me to unload on them, at times, it's not fair because they miss that person, too. My brother missed the guy he used to golf with. My mom missed the guy she could ask about cars. My mother-in-law missed her son. My friends at church missed Chris the funny guy who could always [make them laugh]. If I needed emotional support, sometimes they weren't the ones who needed to give it to me. I unload the big emotional stuff on my therapist."

Sonja Johns speaks from experience when she says, "Don't be afraid to ask for help. Take time to yourself. It's okay to have more underwear than days of the week or month because you don't have to do laundry all the time. I've given up things, like a clean house, but I have happy kids. I look at my house, and it's not spotless. But I have my sewing machine out, and if I did have a spare minute, I would sew. I sew memory quilts for friends. My kids have their toys out, but at least they are playing in here with me. It may be messy in here, but they're playing in here. They're not locked up in their rooms. I give up cooking (most nights making spaghetti, etc.). But I wouldn't give up the person I've become. I would give anything to have Chris back, but I wouldn't give up the person I've become."

photo by Allison Wheeler

24 SHIRLEY SKILES—
THE GREAT GRANDMOTHER

"Nana, you've gotta come to the library. You're the only one I've got."

Great-grandmother Shirley Skiles is the single parent to Alicia (seven) and Andre (five), who were abandoned as infants. At seventy-five, she stepped up to raise two energetic young children when their parents stepped out.

Shirley's story began over fifty years ago at a dance hall in Oklahoma City. "I was celebrating my eighteenth birthday, I guess it was. We both were there [she and her future husband, Carl]. He asked me to dance, and that was it," she chuckles. "That was in March, and we got married in May!"

Shirley and Carl couldn't wait to start a family of their own. After nine years of trying, they adopted a sweet baby girl whom they named Becky. The happy couple hoped to give her the life she could have never had if she had been raised by an alcoholic mother addicted to dope. By sixteen, Becky began the classic struggle of nature versus nurture, finding herself unable to escape the claws of drugs and alcohol which had captured her biological mother. Becky sank into a deep depression while her parents searched for help. "When she started that, that's when we had her tested. We had her with a psychiatrist for a long time." The psychiatrist discovered that Becky was brilliant. "She had a very high IQ" and was also a bi-polar schizophrenic.

"Wilder than the March wind," Becky left home before she graduated high school. Her infrequent trips home to beg for cash to feed her addictions were the only way Carl and Shirley knew where she was.

Out of the three children Becky bore later on, her son Seth stayed the closest to his grandparents, whose home became a safe haven during his teenage years. His mother signed over custody of him to Shirley and Carl because she was unable to provide for his most basic needs.

When Seth had a daughter of his own, Alicia, he and the mother of his child (his on-again, off-again girlfriend Cari) stayed with Shirley and Carl until the responsibilities of parenting became more than they could bear. When Carl and Shirley woke up one morning, the couple and all of their belongings were gone. The only thing left was a crib, with six-month-old baby Alicia still in it.

Seth and Cari returned years later with Andre, Cari's five-month-old son from another relationship. Carl and Shirley took the family in, and just like before, the parents left under the cover of darkness. At sixty-eight and seventy, Shirley and Carl became the proud parents of a six-month-old baby boy. Andre developed a special bond with his great grandfather. Shirley remembers fondly, "He was attached to Carl. Every step Carl took, he took," until Carl's very last.

After fifty-two years of marriage, Carl died at the age of seventy-two. "My last words to him were, 'The babies and I will be okay, and we love you.'"

At seventy, Shirley became a single parent to her two great-grandchildren,

Alicia (four at the time) and Andre (age two). Shirley believes more grandparents are raising their grandchildren because "there are more drugs, alcohol, and pressure than we ever had. I think parents and teachers push them too hard. I think now there are two parents working. No one is there for the kids." Meanwhile, Shirley Skiles is standing in the gap.

During a time in life when most people are filling their days with late breakfasts, relaxing afternoons, and hours of recreation, Shirley sits back in her weathered recliner and lifts her frail finger to point out how she finds the energy to raise two young children. "I know what I have to do. I have to get them to school. I have to get them fed. I don't have to clean the house," her raspy laugh giving away her age. "We do homework. We have a snack. Then after that they curl up in my lap, in my chair, and they'll fall asleep. Later I'll make dinner, and we'll go to bed."

In the absence of her late husband Carl, Shirley finds joy in "having that little girl say, 'I love you,' and that little boy give me a hug," she whispers pointing to Alicia and Andre playing at her feet. "I want them to be happy," which is why she makes it a point to be at every school event. When Alicia says, "Nana, you've got to come to the library. You're the only one I've got," Shirley knows this is true.

While she yearns for the day she'll see Carl again, she fights for each new day knowing she can't leave this world as long as her great-grandchildren need her. "Sometimes I have to leave them at another family member's house, and Andre will say, 'Nana, you're going to be back right? You're not going to leave me forever are you?' And I say, 'No, I'm coming back. I won't leave you.'"

photo by Sherry Lynch Photography/OKC

25 RHONDA THOMAS— BLAZING A TRAIL, IMPACTING THE WORLD

Rhonda Thomas is a trailblazer. Against the advice of her church, she divorced from her abusive husband, leaving behind all she had ever known. That's when she began her own organization to support single parents because "there was nothing available in the place where you're supposed to feel the safest, which is the church."

For years, Rhonda suffered silently in what could only be described as a violent marriage. "I remember one day, I was almost strangled to death. I went to the chiropractor because I was in so much pain. He asked me what happened, and I lied."

Rhonda spent years more afraid of the shame that stemmed from divorce than the brutality of her husband's abuse. "We were at a church where divorce is not an option. I grew up in a family, very close knit, where no one ever got a divorce. So for me the thought of a divorce was traumatic not just family-wise, but from a religious standpoint, too."

The strength to leave came after the birth of her son Nathan, when someone she loved gave her permission to leave. Pain streams down through the tears in her eyes as Rhonda recalls, "The level of stress was huge. My dad came for Christmas that week. My [now] ex came home and became agitated when he saw me serving my dad food, so an argument ensued. My dad confronted me, and I finally just told him everything. He said, 'You don't have to do this anymore.'" That was the moment when Rhonda decided to leave.

In her church at the time, Rhonda's divorce "was the unpardonable sin. You get looked upon like you have a disease. If you're in a circle of couples, then you don't belong anymore. In fact, it's easier for you to go away so they don't have to deal with you, which I did."

Rejection taught Rhonda grace. "It took me a while to work my way out of the religious jungle," where "I was chief," she says laughing. "Please don't take me wrong when I say this. I go to church, but I am very anti-religion. I'm against people's limited view as to how things should be." It took her so long to get a divorce because she was "trying to sort through that whole thing about how 'you're going to hell,' if you get a divorce, or 'you're worthless,' and people treat you that way. It took me ten years to work through all of the religious garbage. I call it garbage not because I'm trying to be disrespectful, but because I have the understanding that man in his best efforts can only act in the light of what he knows." Now Rhonda knows that "their list of do's and don'ts is an effort to have you conform to something that looks like Christianity in their brains."

Although Rhonda left the church for a while, she never left God. "There was a lot of healing that happened just from praising and music. I sought counseling and went to sessions through the YWCA [Young Women's Christian Association]. It has been huge to watch, just to see how if we allow God to move what can happen."

Rhonda says, "I've asked 'why?' a lot since I was a small child. Now I ask 'what?'"

In 2005, she got her answer: The Single Parent Support Network (SPSN).

"It started out of a personal need. I wanted to do this, but from a Christian perspective. Our main objective here is to draw people in to begin to heal and move to another level. When you heal the parent, you heal the family."

SPSN started out as a place where single parents could come together as a community to support and uplift each other by carrying one another's burdens. "We began with just one event called Queen for a Day, an annual all-expenses-paid day of pampering and educating single parents with childcare provided. From there we began support groups, then a monthly parents night out, and even life coaching. Our next goal is partnering with employers to bridge the gap between successful employees and successful business" by offering help and healing to the single parents who work for them.

Rhonda uses SPSN to pass on the wisdom she has gained from her experience as a single parent. She tells all of their members, "The most important thing is having a family plan. This is a clearly articulated vision statement that defines your family's goals, values, and guiding principles for the future. Ours is: 'Blazing a trail, impacting the world.' Everything we do is filtered through that vision,"—a vision that is changing the world one single parent at a time.

Rhonda Thomas continues to lead SPSN fearlessly into uncharted territory as she works non-stop to take this organization nationwide. She and her son Nathan are very close and have been commissioned to blaze trails and move into uncharted territory for generations to come.

26 MARTHA'S HOUSE— A HOUSE FULL OF LOVE

In a rundown neighborhood in downtown Oklahoma City, a two-story red brick house with a big white porch stands between seven families and homelessness. Martha's House, as it is called, provides transitional housing for single-parent families who would otherwise be on the street.

Sometimes, people need a second chance. Or a third. Or a fourth.

Nicole (not her real name), a petite, beautiful, young mother is getting that chance.

With her three adorable children under five playing at her feet in their tiny apartment, she tells of the difficulty of trying to find employment without childcare and a felony conviction for marijuana possession hanging over her head. "It's very disheartening: trying and trying and nothing works."

In her short life, Nicole has born more heartache than one might think her slender shoulders could bear. She married her first love at nineteen, but their tumultuous relationship ended when he returned from Iraq and abandoned her and her young son leaving them homeless in Colorado. She slept for months on a friend's couch, worked two jobs, and hardly ever got to see her baby. So when he was eight months old, she made the tearful decision to give her son up for adoption. "I wanted to give him a life," she says. "I don't regret it at all when I see how he has thrived and flourished with his family, but I shut down emotionally after that."

Her second son's father was a hustler who sold marijuana. "I was smoking weed all the time." When she found out she was pregnant, she left Colorado for Oklahoma to "get away from that lifestyle and all that negativity" and moved in with an old friend from high school. She stayed for two years and had her daughter London. The friend turned out to be "crazy violent" and was convicted of assault and child abuse for picking up her young son and throwing him to the ground in a fit of rage. While the friend was in jail, Nicole packed up their things, and they moved into a shelter, the YMCA.

After a month there, she signed a lease on a house that turned out to be uninhabitable with mold, sewer problems, mice, and roaches. When she approached Legal Aid for assistance in getting out of the lease, they directed her to Martha's House. She was selected from among the dozens of inquiries they receive each month to live in one of their seven apartments for a small program fee for up to two years. After moving in, despite being on birth control, she discovered she was pregnant again.

Thankfully, living in a big house and providing your kids with all the latest toys aren't on Nicole's checklist for what makes a successful parent. "I will be completely proud if they like school and want to go to the library. Teaching them to have that desire to learn makes me happier than anything."

In fact, Nicole believes that a life of ease and material wealth isn't always a better life. "I attended Air Academy High School in Colorado. All these rich kids with BMWs and Jaguars had everything handed to them," she recalls. "They made fun of me and the other military kids without very much at all. They still brag about everything they have. But in my head, that's nothing to be proud of. The trials and tribulations of life are what build you to be who you are. They mold your character and make you stronger. God forbid something happens to their parents, what are they going to do? I think their parents are doing them a disservice by handing everything to them."

Despite being rejected for hundreds of jobs and her time running out at Martha's House, Nicole is optimistic. "I have started my own business doing personal organization, personal concierge services, and event planning." She calls her business "The Gift of Time."

"I have a lot of dreams. I have always wanted to be an entrepreneur," she says. "It's not always going to be like this. I'm going to provide for them and more, but the best parents go above and beyond, enriching their lives with more than just material things."

Nicole even dreams of operating her own women's shelter someday, "maybe in a large house or old hotel with a common kitchen and living room to encourage people to come out of their rooms and not huddle in their own apartments all day—and a large common computer area." Her heart goes out to other single parents who, like herself, have no support network, "A lot of folks call themselves single moms, but they live with their parents or grandparents. You don't have your child's father there with you, but you have all these other people there helping you."

The love and patience that Nicole shows with her children has not gone unnoticed in the home bursting with moms and children. A staff member, Tera Yacobacci, confirmed what anyone could guess from a few hours with the soft-spoken mom and her babies, "She never yells at them. She always has them with her. She's not eager to leave them with anyone else. She makes sure they eat healthy and are polite."

Nicole's example filters through their whole family. "It touches my heart and makes me cry tears of happiness how they interact with each other and love each other. It gives me chills inside," says Nicole. "When London was born, she was in NICU for a while. When Jackson first saw her, he started crying and loving on her and said, 'My baby! My baby!' He was instantly nurturing towards his baby sister. With this baby as well," she says of the nursing infant in her arms. "They both love her, and are all into her, and play with her. Jackson teaches his sisters a lot. He's more patient than me sometimes. That's the one thing I love most: how close they are to each other. Maybe that's because my family and I weren't that close, it makes it that much more special that they are close."

Some may look at families in their big houses and parents with great careers and call them a success. Nicole's future may be uncertain, and she may not have many worldly possessions to pass on to her children, but she believes she is giving them something worth far more—a house full of love.

Martha's House is a ministry of the Neighborhood Service Organization, a faith-based organization founded by Methodist women that serves at-risk and homeless populations in Oklahoma City by providing housing solutions and teaching skills to transform lives.

photo by Bryan Crump

27 JOYCE SIMMONS—
EMPTY NEST, FULL LIFE

Joyce still vividly remembers the afternoon her world fell apart. "I came home after work and was getting stuff ready for dinner. My husband was sitting at the counter with a pen in one hand and papers in the other hand. He told the boys to go upstairs to play; then he said, 'I want a divorce.' At thirty-five, he left me for an eighteen-year-old."

When Joyce Simmons' husband left her for a "newer model" twenty-five years ago, she poured her heart and soul into raising her two boys, David and Brad. But now that they are grown, she hasn't stopped the outpouring of love—just changed the recipients.

"God put me on this earth to spread His Word and His love. Now it's time for me to give back."

At the time, her sons were ages four and five. Bitterness came easy then. But today Joyce recommends, "Show the kids as little as possible. Don't argue in front of the kids. Don't complain about your spouse. It's tough not to, but I would have tried harder if I had it to do over again."

She credits her sons with pulling her through her most difficult days. "You can't stay in bed when you have to get up and take care of them. They are my saving grace. They made me stronger because I had to be strong for them."

Now she volunteers with several ministries that support single moms, and she tells them, "Put your own wants, needs, and desires aside, and show your kids as much unconditional love as you can while you have them with you. Sooner or later, they are going to grow up and be gone. My sons tell me about the sacrifices I made. I don't even remember. They remember. When the world tears them apart, they don't think about the things they didn't have. They think about the fact that they have one place where one person is always going to love them and accept them."

Joyce believes God protected her boys even more than she realized at the time. When they were young, the boys started acting out in school. Some "wonderful" people took an interest in them and helped set up several months of free counseling through the United Way. "They just blossomed after that. There were no more behavioral problems in school. I remember the last session, walking out with Brad and praying, 'God, when the kids grow up I will do everything I can for You because You've done everything for my kids.'"

Even though they had a few bumps in the road, she could still see God's hand on their lives—like when her youngest son David at age fifteen was arrested for being out past curfew. He snuck out of the house after she was asleep and went joyriding in her car with his two friends.

What most parents would consider a terrible moment, Joyce saw as a teachable one. "It was probably the best thing that could have ever happened to that young man. He had to go to court. The judge gave him community service. He had to write a paper on the Bill of Rights. The most significant thing was that she made him take a tour of the Oklahoma County Jail. I can remember David coming home that day and saying, 'Mom, I'm so sorry I did what I did, and I will never do anything like that again because I don't want to ever, ever go in there, ever.' I'm telling you, that was it. I never had problems with that kid after that. Nothing. Not a thing."

When Joyce promised God that she would do everything she could to help

Him once her kids were grown, she meant it. In addition to her full-time job as a paralegal in a downtown law firm, she packs her schedule full with volunteering opportunities. "I love it. I love all of it. I like to help people. It gives me joy."

Her volunteerism at church started when the boys' youth pastor asked her if she would consider teaching. "Me? Who had never owned a Bible until I started coming to church with my boys? He knew I was a newbie, but he took a chance on me." She taught in the church youth group for years ("until I turned fifty and couldn't understand what they were saying anymore.").

She says, "Because [that youth pastor] took a chance on me, I've been able to go up to others and ask, 'Have you ever thought about helping here?' Because someone else had faith in me, it makes it easier for me to go up and ask them."

She currently teaches first and second grade Sunday School ("they are the most precious things God has put on the earth"). She also facilitates Bible studies.

In addition, Joyce is in charge of an enormous clothing exchange organized by her church. "We give clothes away twice a year. The congregation brings the clothing. Literally, the cafeteria is just packed with clothes, just packed full. People come in droves and walk out with bags of clothes, coats, shoes and toys. People give so generously."

She feels strongly about single moms supporting one another and volunteers with both Arise Ministries and the Single Parent Support Network. "[Single parents] need encouragement. You need to be with other parents who are raising their kids by themselves. It's important to have a base where you can go for encouragement, for attachment. It's hard to get single moms to make that first step to go to ministries like that, but once they do, they are hooked."

"People need a lot of help, and I like to help. I just do. If God has given me the ability to do things, then I shouldn't just sit on my rump and not do them. He put me on the earth to spread the Word about Him and His love. It would be selfish not to give back. I know that I was blessed by a lot of people. It's time for me to give back. I made that promise to Him.

"I'd do anything for my boys, and they'd do anything for me. But I never felt this empty nest stuff [after they left]. There are different seasons of your life. I gave my children everything I could give while they were with me. But now it's time for them to fly, and it's time for me to fly as well."

Joyce works for an attorney in downtown Oklahoma City and, after twenty-five years of apartment living, resides in a quaint home near her office that she purchased a year ago. Brad served in the U.S. Army during the war in Iraq. He is now married and recently received his certified public accountant (CPA) license. David has a successful career in sales and still calls his mom every day.

28 JAN DUNHAM –
THE MIRACLE WORKER

"This is what the LORD says: 'Your wound is incurable, your injury beyond healing. There is no one to plead your cause, no remedy for your sore, no healing for you. But I will restore you to health and heal your wounds,' declares the LORD. 'Because you are called an outcast...for whom no one cares." Jeremiah 30:12-13, 17

Jan Dunham is the Oklahoma director of the Children's Miracle Network Hospitals, an organization raising funds to help children who suffer from common childhood afflictions, birth defects, and/or disease. With Jan's help, the Children's Miracle Network Hospitals provide comfort, treatment, and hope, to millions of sick kids each year. If you don't recognize the name, maybe you'll recognize their logo—a simple, child-like drawing of a hot air balloon that floats like hope over the clouds. Jan Dunham knows all about clouds.

A dark cloud hung over Jan's and her daughter's heads for many years. "I was the wife not wanted," recalls Jan. "She was the daughter not wanted." Long after separating from her alcoholic husband, to whom she stayed married for twenty painful years, she still struggles to understand how "he could walk away from his own children."

Jan thought the divorce would be a wake-up call to her now ex-husband, to get the help he needed so that he could become the father her children deserved. But instead, he disappeared completely from their lives leaving a deep wound that no amount of therapy could heal. Her two children, daughter Anje (fourteen at the time) and son Brian (eighteen) were heartbroken.

Twelve years after her divorce, Jan began working for the Children's Miracle Network Hospitals because she was passionate about helping children, but after all that time she still felt helpless to fix her own. Knowing how earnestly a daughter longs for the love of her father, she did everything she could to reconcile her husband to her kids when he disowned them after the divorce. No matter how hard she tried it became obvious that, "one person can't be both," so "I did the best I could." Her best efforts never felt good enough.

When all seemed lost, providence led Jan to bump into an old friend. After a brief conversation he said, "You know, you're still complaining about the same things you were complaining about a year ago. Don't you think you need to get on with your life?" Instead of discouraging her, his comments were an "Aha!" moment for Jan.

"Okay, stop it!" she told herself. "Stop living in the past. No longer be a victim, but be a victor." She admits, "It's so hard to do, but when you come to the realization that you are being weighed down by the past, you can conquer. You can move on. The past doesn't have to define you. You can be a different person, and you can be victorious. Sometimes when you're rejected and told your whole life that you aren't good enough, you start believing it. You come out of it believing, 'If he didn't want me, no one else will want me.' I knew I was tired of telling this story, but I guess I kept looking for someone else to give me the answer. I realized I had to be the answer. I had to make the change."

Even after this epiphany, Jan was still trying mend her daughter's broken heart. A few years ago, as a last ditch effort "I emailed my ex-husband, encouraging him to reconnect with his children," who were haunted by the rejection of their still-absent father, but that turned out to be a useless plea.

Jan finally came to the conclusion, "I was trying too hard to fix things rather than focus on Anje." From then on Jan says, "I've just wrapped my arms around her and loved her. I trusted her, believed in her. She was thankful for that. I told her I would never, ever, leave her."

"Anje relied on her faith and trusted the Lord to get through it. She and I are very close. Anje has turned forty now, she is beautiful, happy, and has lots of friends. Brian got married and has four wonderful children of his own."

What makes Jan and the network she represents miraculous isn't the medical conditions getting fixed, it's the people, like her, who willingly carry another child's burdens as if it were their own. "God is showing me that I can be strong and that everything is possible through Him. Life is so much better now than it used to be. Things are happy now, there's not a cloud."

Jan Dunham is now happily married to Dennis Dunham, her husband of nineteen years. Brian and Anje love him, and they continue to have a close bond and relationship with their mom.

29 CARLA HINTON—
OVERCOMING THE STIGMA OF DIVORCE

"I hate it when I hear people get divorced in less than one year, and yet I hung in there way past the point I should have." Overcoming the stigma tied to divorce proved to be challenging for *The Oklahoman's* religious editor, Carla Hinton. "I thought that things would turn around, I thought if I prayed hard enough, but it just didn't."

"As a divorced person I felt branded, I felt shame. There was definitely a big sense of failure. It took me years. It took faith more than time to overcome that, latching onto scriptures that told me what God thought about me rather than what society tells a person who is divorced and a mother of three."

"Sometimes I think single parents put that burden on ourselves. Because there are some people out there who just see you as a person."

To illustrate her point, Carla tells of packing a picnic dinner and taking her kids to a park with a duck pond in their new neighborhood. As a couple approached, she thought, "Oooh, what are they gonna say or do to us?" In fact, they only wanted to give Carla their bread crumbs to feed the ducks. "I think I felt a burden that maybe other people didn't have, you know, at first. I felt like I had a big *D* on the top of my head, *Divorced*, that everyone else could see."

For a little while, Carla traded her *D* for a *W*. "For me as a single person, I put a lot of energy into my work. It was like, if I fail at this one thing [marriage], I'm gonna make up for it over here [at work]." Before her divorce Carla says, "To be honest with you, as an unhappily married person, I don't think I was the best employee I could be. I was a better employee as a single person who was out of that bad marriage. I couldn't focus. I would worry about what I was coming home to." Despite excelling at work, Carla still felt bad.

"A lot of people think that if you had a bad marriage you don't feel bad after [divorcing]. But as a lot of single parents know, especially when you have kids, you are still connected with that person for life. You have to figure out how to parent. First of all, you have to put the kids first." Getting divorced helped Carla to not only become a better employee, "but, I realized that I was a better parent, too."

Not only did Carla have to overcome her own judgments, but the church's as well. With a complicated marriage behind her and a booming writing career in front of her, Carla was steadfast in her efforts to build a better future for her kids. Their family traveled from town to town for her kids' sporting events. After missing a few Sundays as a result of her daughter's basketball games, Carla returned to church where they heard a sermon targeted at her family. "Specifically they said, there are people who have abandoned their ministry, and basketball is not your ministry!" Saddened by the lack of understanding, Carla and her family left that church and found another.

"A good parent is focused on their child's well-being. A great parent is willing to make sacrifices for their well-being. As a good parent, we get legalistic and think, 'My house has to be cleaned by a certain time, and this is for my child's well-being.' Maybe that night you forgo washing the dishes, and you just read a story because maybe they just need more time with you. If you focus on what their need is at that particular time, then it is going to be okay. It is going to be different every day." Every day there is a challenge to overcome.

Carla's willingness to single-handedly taxi her three children to three different kinds of sporting events year-round paid off. All three of her kids received sports scholarships: her oldest for football, her middle child for basketball, and her youngest for track.

Carla's mantras became "I am fearfully and marvelously made" from the Psalms and "I am more than a conqueror" from Romans. Although she had gained faith in herself, God had to teach her to overcome her lack of faith in Him. "I had a hard time trusting Him to meet my needs."

Carla got the chance to test her faith when her ex-husband lost his job and couldn't pay child support. "To say things were tight is putting it mildly.

There wasn't any money for any extras, absolutely not. Our only treat for two weeks was when I would take them to McDonald's on payday, and I would get them Happy Meals. That was it. That was our extra."

Things became so tight that she couldn't even afford to do that. She cried out, "God, is this what it's come down to? I can't even buy the kids cookies. We don't have anything sweet."

Later that day they went to an event where one of her kids won a huge container of no-bake cookies in a cake walk. "We ate on them for days, almost a week. I had just prayed for that! I know that sounds silly. I know that was God. He's, I don't know, He's interested even in our little things. It was like God was saying, 'I hear you, I know what you're going through, and here's something just for you.'"

"That's what single parents have to remember, that He is even there in the little things. It's hard for us. I think so many single parents, we get out of focus. As women we get out of focus and think, 'I need to find a man.' I say, 'No, you have a man; you have Jesus. Let him take care of your needs.'"

God is still taking care of Carla's needs, and she is still writing about it. To read Carla Hinton's inspirational words, you can find her stories in the religious section of *The Oklahoman*.

30 CLAUDIA WINKLER ANDERSON—
THE RICHNESS OF FAMILY

Should you ever be privileged enough to receive an invitation to a dinner party at Claudia Anderson's home or any of her three sisters' homes—go. The only thing more lovely than the elegant but simple fare will be the sparkling wit, genteel manners, frequent laughter, fascinating stories, and the love and joy their family obviously feels in each other's company.

Claudia and her Washington, D.C.-based clan of four sisters is so tightly knit that her son Tom says he feels he was "raised by committee." He remembers, "The way we grew up in our family, we were always around a lot of adults." He adds, "We went to a lot of dinner parties and were comfortable with a lot of different people from an early age. We were a very creative, active family. It was a huge blessing to have come from that environment. I didn't understand until I was older the lengths to which my mother went to create those experiences with the rest of the family."

Indeed. As single parents know, when providing for your children alone, nothing comes easy.

Claudia's journey as a single parent began when she got pregnant "by someone I didn't want to marry, someone I considered unsuitable for marriage." Despite her misgivings, she was young and thought she could do whatever she set her mind to, so she married and moved with him to England. A few short years into their marriage and a second child later, she realized her mistake and left.

For Claudia, the hardest thing about being a single mother "was feeling exiled forever from a 'whole' family—father, mother, child—knowing we could never have that. If I ever got remarried, we'd have a different kind of family. We were torn—a fragment, you know. That always grieved me and weighed heavily on me, both for myself and the kids. For years after I left Richard, when I saw a father walking down the street with a child, I would cry. Not only were they apart from their father, but he was such a difficult father for them to build a relationship with or to love."

Her daughter, Hilary, echoed that sentiment and wished her mother had protected them even more from their father when they were young. "It was very scary," she says tearfully of her father's calls or their few visits. "She never explained to us he was an alcoholic or mentally ill. All the emphasis was on the fact he was our father, so we had to go see him. There was never an indication that he had a responsibility to act better." She recommends that parents, "at least explain to the child that the person is impaired. It would have been much better if we had that armor. Make it clear that the child is the priority, not him."

But while their nuclear family would never be exactly what Claudia had once envisioned, she made every effort to make sure they were part of a big, secure extended family. "The best thing about being a single parent was the way my sisters rallied around and made my children part of their families. It helped them grow in social skills, but I just loved that they knew they were part of a big family where they were loved and that they could count on. That was very precious."

After leaving England, Claudia and her children (ages three and one at the time) moved in with her mother on Capitol Hill in Washington, D.C. where they lived for the next seven years. While providing them a home, her mother worked long hours as a journalist, so she did not help with babysitting. "She wanted her freedom to come and go," remembers Claudia.

Claudia, trying to think of ways to make money while being at home with her children, became a freelance editor. Despite the lonely, solitary work, she emphasizes, "The fact that there was nothing in my life except work and children for many years was not something that I fought as some people might. I loved taking care of them." She even credits the singular focus of caring for her children with saving her from "adolescent despair." She adds, "Sometimes we can't tell when God is giving us a great gift. Sometimes it seems like a catastrophe at the time."

One of her favorite memories of their childhood was "reading to them in bed, me in the middle and one on each side. There were some books we'd read, and when we got to the end, they would insist we start over again. I mean long books like *Huckleberry Finn*. I read them a children's *Iliad* and *Odyssey*. They loved it. When it was over, I said, 'Now kids, I want to read you a poem. You may hate it, but just let me read it to you.' I wanted to read them the marvelous Keats sonnet about reading Homer for the first time. It is a beautiful poem. It ends in this stirring way with Cortez discovering the Pacific Ocean, like 'My god, another ocean!' The kids were transfixed; and when I finished, they said, 'Read it again!' Here I was thinking I was inflicting something on them. That was a nice moment," she laughs.

When Tom and Hilary were nine and eleven, they left Washington, D.C. for Claudia's first newspaper job in Buffalo, New York. "It was a great adventure." But the paper went out of business within six months, so they had to move again, to Cincinnati, Ohio.

Her job on the editorial page there was "extremely demanding, but very fun and interesting." They approached it as a team. Claudia laughs, "I'll never forget when I first joined the newspaper, Tom tore an article out of *Time* magazine and folded it up and gave it to me and said, 'Mom, I thought you might find this interesting.' It was all about inflation! It was such a dear gesture!"

But there were also challenges of being alone in a new city. On her very first day of her new job, Claudia had every single parent's nightmare: a sick child with no childcare options.

"We had just moved, so we knew only one person," recalls Claudia. "I had some sense that as a woman you had to be twice as good. One thing you couldn't do was say, 'Because I'm a mother, I can't come to work.' So I called up the one neighbor who had reached out and invited us over for dinner and said, 'Is there any way I can bring this sick child to you?' And she said, 'Sure. Bring him over.' I put him to bed in her bed, and I went to work. It was awful."

Tom, however, says that as a child, he didn't think anything was amiss. He trusted his mother's decisions. "We were raised as part of the group, not in charge. You knew your place. Children weren't making the decisions. We understood the intrinsic authority that comes from parents." He adds that "We weren't confined by a lot of rules, but there was an expectation of responsible behavior."

The seven years away from their extended family in Washington were hard. "Newspapers go 365 days a year. So I wasn't available a lot of the time. I had to work a lot of holidays," she recalls. "But it was wonderful to be able to send them to my sisters." Hilary and Tom spent holidays and summers during those years back in D.C. or in Nantucket with their aunt, uncles, and cousins. They were the oldest of the ten grandchildren and as Claudia says, "Their cousins looked up to them and worshipped them."

Eventually, Claudia was promoted to chief editorial writer for Scripps Howard newspapers, the chain that owned the *Cincinnati Post*, and they moved back to the D.C. area.

"I was really under a LOT of strain in that job," emphasizes Claudia. "But I got to write about all this amazing history—the unraveling of communism, the fall of the Soviet Union. It was thrilling, but it was also terrifying because my work had a potential audience of two million people if you added up all the readers of every paper. There wasn't a lot of latitude for making mistakes."

A year after the move back to the Washington area, Hilary went to college.

Although Tom spent a lot of time on his own, he says he never felt abandoned. "Our family was so important to me—all the aunts, uncles and cousins—that I never wanted what other kids [from two-parent families] had."

In 1995, Claudia's life started to change significantly. In the space of two months, she likes to say she "got a new house [on Capitol Hill], a new job [at *The Weekly Standard*], and a new body [hysterectomy]." That was also the beginning of a long, deep inner transformation that culminated in her baptism in 1998. Instrumental in this was a Bible study initiated by one of her new neighbors, Pastor Mark Dever of Capitol Hill Baptist Church.

Her new faith opened her eyes to some of her blind spots as a parent. "I changed my thinking so much after my children left home," she says. "I had been fixated on my children's role in *my* life. I failed to appreciate adequately that they were individuals in their own right temporarily entrusted to my care. Your child is not your creation or your possession. He is a unique individual who belongs to God."

But her words of hard-learned wisdom and advice ring true for all parents:

"Grow in self-knowledge, because the more you understand your strengths and weaknesses, the better you will be able to compensate. Be grateful for your strengths and employ them well, but understand your limitations and find ways to compensate for them. "

"Teach them the most important things: to love God and love your neighbor. To love truth and to be brave in standing up for it in whatever way life may require you to."

And finally, words that sound strange coming from one who strove so hard for so long:

"We are told in the Bible so many times to aspire to a simple life. It is enough if you can be faithful and love and serve those around you. Maybe some of the striving is beside the point. Let go."

Claudia is now the managing editor of *The Weekly Standard* and lives in a row house on Capitol Hill with her new husband Bill, only blocks from two of her sisters and her daughter.

Hilary married her soulmate (on what Claudia says was "the happiest day of my life") and is completing her third year as a nurse in the transplant unit at Georgetown University Hospital.

Tom is an F-18 pilot who has done a tour with the Blue Angels and will soon embark on his fifth deployment as a commander of F-18s. In January 2013, he married a lovely young lady as accomplished and interesting as the rest of their remarkable family.

31 JIM BOZE—
HEALING AROUND THE DINNER TABLE

Jim Boze lost forty-six pounds in six weeks when his wife left him; he knows what it means to grieve. His wife went to a rehab center for help with her prescription drug addiction, met someone, and returned only to pack her things, leaving him to raise their three children, Tonia (eleven), David (ten), and Doug (five).

But he also knows what it means to laugh. You can hardly speak to Jim without at least cracking a smile at his constant wit. His oldest son has even made a career from the family love of entertaining and humor as a popular drive-time talk radio host of The David Boze Show in Seattle.

You would never guess amidst the lively dinner table banter of this happy family that it was ever anything less than the American dream. In fact, keeping consistent meal times at the dinner table was one of the things Jim insisted on, even in the midst of struggling to work and raise three kids by himself. He only half-jokingly says he would like to write *The Single Dad*

Cookbook to help dads make home-cooked meals for their kids and also give parenting tips.

When asked what he did best as a single parent, he quips, "I married Barbara." But in a more serious vein, he offers the encouragement that, "you can be a single parent and have a happy family as well as a two-[parent family]. It's just more work. I don't know where you get the rest. You don't get to share the load or the burdens—financial burdens, or sick kids, or whatever it might be."

Jim was introduced to Barbara by her cousin who could see they thought so much alike that they would be a perfect match. She's been proven right. Jim and Barb rounded out the family with three more children: Colleen, Johnny, and Jimmy. The love between the siblings is evident, and a newcomer would never know they are a blended family. "We never treated any of the kids differently. We introduced them all as 'our kids.' They never heard any distinction from us."

Part of Jim's parenting philosophy is that kids don't need to be entertained. "I like to see them use their own imaginations." As part of that philosophy, they haven't had TV since the kids were little. "I was painting the house, and I cut a wire that held up the antenna. I never put it back on. From that point on, we didn't have TV."

Sometimes those active imaginations could be a double-edged sword.

His daughter, Tonia, who perhaps suffered the most from her mother's leaving, struggled during her teenage years. "I was blessed enough to catch her whenever she tried to sneak out, so I think she thought I had super powers," says Jim. "But the fact is, I made nearly every mistake a kid could, and nothing prepared me for being a parent better than past experience."

But when asked about favorite memories, Jim focuses on the present, not the past. "The best times are when the families are together telling stories. They are all good storytellers. And we all have good senses of humor. We enjoy sitting around the table listening to the kids talk about their lives and all the things we didn't know about at the time. They feel safe telling us now twenty years later."

A lot of those stories involve Tonia's driving. One morning, David read in the newspaper about someone damaging a car in the local grocery store parking lot then leaving the scene followed in hot pursuit by the car's owner, not knowing he was reading about his own sister's exploits the night before. On another occasion, Jim walked outside to see their Buick scratched from bumper to bumper and missing chrome like it had gone through a tunnel too small for the car. Tonia tried to brush off the damage with "it should be fine. I think you can buff it out."

"They weren't so funny then, but they are funny now," Jim chuckles.

For single parents in the midst of raising kids (or teenage rebellion), he says, "I can only offer the advice that everyone gives and that you don't believe at the time: time does heal. It does get better."

The laughter around the dinner table at the Boze house is living proof.

photo by Sam Lamott

32 ANNE LAMOTT—
THE TRUTH TELLER

Best-selling, dearly-loved author and speaker Anne Lamott has been inspiring and encouraging single parents for more than twenty years with the revolutionary but simple act of telling the truth.

From her refreshing, if sometimes raw, honesty in her autobiographical *Operating Instructions: A Journal of My Son's First Year* to the openness with which she shares her struggles with addiction and her spiritual journey, Anne not only gives a voice to the single parent's deepest thoughts and fears, she also offers her experience and faith as a way forward.

"I try to write the books I would love to come upon, that are honest, concerned with real lives, human hearts, spiritual transformation, families, secrets, wonder, craziness—and that can make me laugh. When I am reading a book like this, I feel rich and profoundly relieved to be in the presence of someone who will share the truth with me and throw the lights on a little, and I try to write these kinds of books. Books, for me, are medicine."

Regarding "ideal two-parent" families she shares, "My core belief is that almost all of us are pretty ruined by adulthood, and the lucky ones learn that they are also loved out of all sense of proportion—and the lucky ones can be found in any family, single, gay, adoptive, you name it—where one parent has done the work of personal healing and restoration. Having one well parent is the hugest advantage any child can have."

In the story below, Anne shares the truth about the challenges of raising a teenage son.

Samwheel by Anne Lamott

There are only six stories about Sam at seventeen that he'll allow me to tell, and this is my favorite. It's about a fight we had once that left me wondering whether anyone in history had ever been a worse parent or raised such a horrible child. It challenged my belief that there is meaning to life, and that we are children of divine intelligence and design.

Our fight was ostensibly about the car. We have an old beater that I let Sam drive whenever he wants, although because I pay for the insurance, I have some leverage. It's a good deal for him. But I had taken away his car privileges earlier that week because he'd been driving recklessly, hit a curb going twenty, and destroyed the front tire. So he felt mad and victimized to begin with, my huge, handsome, brown-eyed son. And actually, so did I. I asked him to wash both cars, as partial payment for the tire I'd had to buy. It was a beautiful sunny day, and he had other plans, which I made him postpone. I went for a walk with the dog, to let him work in peace. When I got back, though, the cars were still gauzy with dirt.

I pointed this out, as nicely as possible.

"I washed them," Sam said, defiantly.

"You liar," I said in an affectionate way, because his response was so flagrantly not true I assumed he was joking.

He produced two filthy washrags: "I'm not a liar," he said. "I just did a lousy job." Turning to walk away, he looked back and gave me a catalytic sneer.

It was as if something had tripped a spring-loaded bar in me. And for the first time in our lives, I slapped him on the face.

He didn't flinch—in fact, he barely seemed to register it. He gave me a flat, lifeless look, and I knew I was a doomed human being, and that neither of us could ever forgive me.

Then I grounded him for the night.

I felt I had no choice. Slapping him did not neutralize his culpability: It simply augmented mine.

He looked at me with scorn. "I don't care what you do or don't do anymore," he said. "You have no power over me."

This is not strictly true. He has little money of his own, and loves having our old car to tool around in. Also, he realizes that families are not democracies, and he's smart enough to obey most of the time.

We stood in our driveway looking daggers at each other. The tension was like the air before lightning. The cat ran for her life. The dog wrung her hands.

I felt a wall of tears approaching the shore and, without another thought, got in my car and left. Nothing makes me angrier and more hopeless, than when someone robs me of my reality by trying to gaslight me. Like Charles Boyer with Ingrid Bergman, saying he hadn't seen her purse, when he'd hidden it. Or lowering the gas jets and then pretending not to notice the darkness. I started to cry, hard, and not long after, to keen, like an Irish woman with a son missing at sea.

Recently I have begun to feel that the boy I loved is gone, and in his place, a male person who so pushes my buttons with his moodiness, scorn and flamboyant laziness. People tell me that the boy will return, but some days that is impossible to imagine. And we were doing so well for a while, all those years until his junior year of high school, when the plates of the earth shifted inside him. I've loved and given him so much more than I ever have anyone else, and I'll tell you, a fat lot of good it does these days.

I should not have been driving, but since I'd restricted Sam's driving privileges, I couldn't make him leave. So I drove along, a bib of tears and drool forming on my T-shirt. Why was he sabotaging himself like this, giving up his weekend, his freedom and his car, and for what? Well, I this is what teenagers have to do, because otherwise they would never be able to leave home and go off to become their own people. Kids who are very close to their parents often become the worst shits, and they have to make the parent the villain, so they can break free without having it hurt too much. Otherwise, the parent would have to throw rocks at them to get them out of the house. It would be like a TV wilderness show where the family has nursed the wounded animal back to health, and tries to release it back into the wilds, shooing it away: "Go ahead, Betty! You can fly!"

So even though, or because, I understood this, I cried harder as I drove than I have since my father died. God invented cars to help kids separate from their parents. I have never hated my son so much as when I was teaching him to drive. There, I've said it, I hated him. Sue me: It's actually legal, because sometimes he hates me, too. He always drove too fast, cut corners too sharply, whipping around in the '95 Honda like it was a souped-up Mustang convertible. But somehow, he tricked the California Department of Motor Vehicles into issuing him a license. I hate the way most young men drive, so cocky, reckless, entitled. I suppose they hate the way I drive, too—slow and careful, all but shaking my puny fist at them as they pass.

I started letting Sam drive himself to and from school, and to his appointments, events, practices. I also ordered him to make emergency runs for milk and ice cream sundaes. But recently as he was leaving, I saw him peel around the corner nearest to our home, endangering himself and anyone who might have been on the street. I threatened to take away his driving privileges, and he slowed down. For two days. Then he sped up when he thought I wasn't looking, and lost his rights for a week.

What has happened? Who is this person? He used to be so sane and positive, so proud of himself. He used to call himself "Samwheel" when he was five, because while he couldn't pronounce Samuel, he knew it was a distinguished name. He used to care about everything, but now he mostly only cares about his friends, computers, music, and most hideously, his cell phone—the adolescent's pacemaker. He threatens to run away because he wants his freedom, and the truth is he is too old to be living with me anymore. He wants to have his own house, and hours, and life. He wants my permission to smoke, so he doesn't have to sneak around. He wants to stay out late, and sleep in, and because I won't let him do any of this on weekdays, he sees me as a prig at best and at worst a coldhearted guard at Guantanamo.

I wept at the wheel on a busy boulevard. At first people were looking over at me as they passed in the next lane. I wiped at my face, and snorfled. Then I noticed that people were dropping back. Eventually, there were no cars in my immediate vicinity. I felt like O.J. in his Bronco on that famous ride. I started calling out to God, "Help me! Help me! I'm calling on you! I hate myself, I hate my son!" I wanted to die. What is the point? What if the old bumper sticker is right and the hokey-pokey is what it's all about?

But I have to believe that Jesus prefers honesty to anything else. I was saying, "Here's who I am," and that is where most improvement has to begin.

You've got to wonder what Jesus was like at seventeen. They don't even talk about it in the Bible, he was apparently so awful.

But then I said the stupidest thing: I said, "I'll do anything you say."

Now this always gets Jesus' attention. I could feel him look over, sideways, and steeple his fingers. And smile, that pleased-with-himself smile. "Good," I heard him say. "Now you're talking. So go home already, and deal with it."

So I drove home, wiping at my eyes, and when I stepped inside, Sam said, his voice dripping with contempt, "What do you have to cry about?"

I staggered to my room, like Snagglepuss onstage. I sat on the floor, and thought about his question. The answer was, I didn't have a clue. But all the honest parents I know—all three of them—are in similar straits.

Their kids are mouthy now, and worse; they could care less about school, and some are barely passing. They drive like movie stars from the 50s, like Marlon Brando or Troy Donahue. You can see in their driving that everything in them is raw, too intent, and thoughtless. No wonder teenagers make such good terrorists.

And me? I think the moment Sam was born. I recognized that the things I hated about my parents—their fixation with our doing homework, and getting into a good college; their need to show us off and make us perform socially for their friends—were going to be things Sam hated about me someday. I also knew that I would wreck his life in ways my parents couldn't have even imagined. I knew that God had given me an impossible task, and that I would fail. I knew deep down that life can be a wretched business, and no one, not even Sam, gets out alive.

It turns out that every kid has this one tiny inbred flaw: they have their own skin, their own stains, their own will. Putting aside for a moment the divine truth of their natures, all of them are wrecked, just like the rest of us. That is the fly in the ointment, and this, Sam, is what I had to cry about.

When I finally stopped my sobbing, I called my friend Father Tom, who is actually one of Sam's dear friends, too. I told him my version. He listened.

"You're right on schedule," he said. "And so is he. And I was worse."

"You swear? Thank you! But it's still hopeless," I said. "What should I do?"

"Call the White House and volunteer him for the National Guard."

"Anything else?"

"Let the hard feelings pass. Ask for help. Mary and Joseph had absolutely awful moments, too. See if you can forgive each other a little, just for today. We can't forgive: that's the work of the Spirit. We're too damaged. But we can be willing. And in the meantime, try not to break his fingers."

I sat on my floor and after a while the dog came over and gave me a treatment. Somewhat revived, I tried to figure out the next right thing. It suddenly came to me.

I went and kicked my son's door in.

"Go clean the cars properly," I said. "Now."

And he did, or rather, he hosed them down. Then he went back inside and slammed the door. I went inside and filled a tub with hot soapy water, and took it to him.

"Go wash it again," I said. "With soap, this time. And then rinse it."

I went inside and did everything I could think of that helps when all is hopeless. I ate some yogurt, drank a cool glass of water and cleaned out a drawer. Then I took my nice clean car to the market and bought supplies: the new *People*, a loaf of whole-wheat sourdough, and a jar of raspberry jam. I lay on the couch, read my magazine, and ate toast. Before I started to doze, I turned on CNN softly and watched until I fell asleep.

I woke up a few times. The first time, I was still sad and angry and ashamed, and knew in my heart that things weren't going to be consistently good again for a long time. I was willing for the Spirit to help me forgive myself, and for Sam and me to forgive each other, but these things take time. God does not have a magic wand. Also, I kept my expectations low, which is one of the secrets of life.

Then when I woke up a second time, I saw the last thing on earth I expected to see: Sam in the same room with me, stretched on the other couch, eating yogurt and watching CNN.

"Hi," I said, but he didn't reply. His legs hung over the sides of the couch.

I dozed off again, and when I woke up, he was asleep, the dog on the floor beside him. He was sweating—he always gets hot when he sleeps. He used to nap on this same couch with his head on my legs and ask me to scratch it, and before that he would crawl into bed beside me, and then kick off all the covers, and earlier still, to sleep on my stomach and chest like a hot-water bottle. He and the dog were both snoring. Maybe I had been too, all of us tangled up in one another's dreams.

Everything in the room stirred: dust and light, dander and fluff, the air—my life still in daily circulation with this guy I have been resting with for so many years.

Anne and Sam survived his teenage years, are closer than ever, and have even collaborated on her latest memoir about her grandson Jax, *Some Assembly Required: A Journal of My Son's First Son.*

33 ADRIANNA IWASINSKI— WHAT DOESN'T KILL YOU MAKES YOU STRONGER

Today, Adrianna Iwasinski is living her dream and providing for her two children as an award-winning television journalist. As the Crime Tracker reporter for KWTV, the local CBS affiliate, her face and voice are broadcast across the state every day.

But only five short years ago, her life looked very different. After the death of her mother-in-law, her husband spiraled into addictive behaviors and mental illness. She struggled to save her marriage while also caring full-time for her elderly father-in-law and holding back the threat of the financial ruin caused by her husband's behavior and gambling debts.

"On the surface, we were the perfect family with the beautiful house, the two pretty children, who went to church every Sunday, and everything was rosy," she says. But soon the secrets swept under the rug would bring the whole façade crumbling down.

"Financially, I suffered the worst fate you can face," she says of the crumbling of their family business, the bank foreclosing on their home, and filing for bankruptcy.

Her ex-husband has chosen to no longer have a relationship with her or their children. "I got married for all the right reasons and had children for all the right reasons, but I got divorced for the right reasons, too," she says of her husband who refused to get help after he began abusing prescription drugs and ran up a $40,000 gambling debt in two months. He fought the divorce "tooth and nail," but now that the divorce is final, he no longer has contact with his children. "We don't know where he is. We don't know if he's living under a bridge or remarried and has a happy life. We just don't know," says Adrianna. Even his extended family has turned their backs on her and won't return her phone calls.

Yet spiritually, in the midst of the trials, Adrianna hasn't just survived, she has thrived. "I'm doing something I love. We don't have debt. Do we own a house? No, but it's not the end of the world not to own a house. Everything is on God's timetable. I have that faith now, but I didn't used to."

"It's amazing the village of people who God puts in your life," she says. "We have a village of people who love us and support us. My church provides a scholarship, so my kids can go to Catholic school. I still pay, but the scholarship makes it possible. There is a wonderful man at the church who has become my kids' godfather. He gives the kids a great example of a man who cares for their well-being and mine, but there is no romantic interest. He's older and has kind of taken us under his wing, and we have provided a family for him that he's wanted now that his son is grown."

"I get my grounding from church every week," says Adrianna of her new church. "I'm one of those who likes to get down on my knees and pray and thank God for his blessings. Now, I don't go for the social part. I go to find my center and to find peace. I go for the right reasons."

Before her divorce, Adrianna and her husband went to the church his family attended every time the doors were open. But after the divorce, without support from that church, she had to find her own way.

As a seven-year-old growing up in Ohio, she remembered the local Catholic church as "her happy place." So after the divorce, she sought out a small Catholic church called Christ the King. There, she found the support she so desperately needed as a single parent.

"If I didn't have faith, I would be so miserable," says Adrianna.

"We would be on the street," her five-year-old son, Dane, pipes up. "Because He provides everything."

After the divorce, she got a job with Big Brothers, Big Sisters. But when the economy tanked in 2008, she was laid off. She was unemployed for four months. "*Four long painful months,*" she emphasizes. "Looking for work, trying to find the right fit. I would hit my computer every day."

"When I was unemployed, that was the hardest time in my life. I'm college-educated. I had a career. We had a two-million-dollar business. I had a beautiful home. Really? I'm collecting unemployment? At the same time, it didn't destroy me. It humbled me. Oh, it humbled me so much. But I kept at it."

Before she had children, Adrianna had worked for both the local ABC and CBS affiliates as a reporter, a job she had given up to raise a family and work in the family business.

After her long stretch of unemployment, she had decided to move to Texas, when the news director at her former employer, KWTV, called to ask her if she would like to freelance. Within one week, a full-time daytime reporter position opened up. She asked for the opportunity to be considered and was hired.

Three years later, she says, "I'm telling you it was a God thing."

The irony of God providing a job in the career field she loved but had sacrificed for her family is not lost on Adrianna, except now she manages the demanding job in broadcast journalism while raising two young children by herself. But Adrianna says, "As long as you're in something that you're passionate about, that you were made to do, that you feel like you were put on this earth to do, then working is a pleasure. I love going to work. I'm made for this business."

They still have hard moments. "It breaks my heart when Sophia cries and wants to know why her daddy doesn't want to see her," says Adrianna. "I can't do anything to fix it, but I can listen." While some parents might vent their anger for the absent parent, Adrianna tries to protect her children by saying, "Your daddy loves you, but he doesn't know how to love himself. Daddy's sick, and he's trying to get better. And when he gets better, he'll want to be around you. He doesn't want to have you be around him when he's sick.'"

She struggles to maintain her composure. "We pray for him, but I want my kids to know you can find love, joy, and happiness through other people and through going forward. You can't just lament the past. You've got to keep going forward."

"I've learned that sometimes it's going to be painful and life isn't always fair, but you can survive it. Look at them. They are smart, happy, funny kids. We are closer and stronger. They are more self-sufficient. Do I wish they had a relationship with their dad? Yes. But what doesn't kill you makes you stronger. That's always been my motto. I know it's a cliché," she laughs, "But it's true!"

"I don't think I'm a great mom," she says. "But I try. I know I'm the best mom I can be."

Her son overhearing from the other room protests, "You *are* a great mom!"

"Maybe that's the measure," she says softly.

Soon Adrianna's face will be broadcast not only throughout her state, but into millions of homes around the nation, as she participates in a new television reality show scheduled to air in summer 2013.

34 AHSHA MORIN–
BRINGING BLESSINGS FROM A BROKEN HOME

Breaking up a home is sometimes best for everyone, but that doesn't mean it doesn't hurt.

Ahsha Morin says the hardest part about being a single parent is "the pain you put your kids through. You can't hide that; you can't deny that; you can't stop that. Knowing that I have caused some of their pain is the worst part."

She should know. She is the child of a single mother herself.

Ahsha's mother discovered she was pregnant while engaged to her biological father. "He thought it wouldn't look good. He wasn't sure he was ready for children, so he said, 'You better have an abortion.' My mom was like 'No Way.' If she had not been strong enough to stand up for what she believed in, I wouldn't be sitting here right now," says Ahsha. "I definitely got some of her strength—to be able to walk away from that relationship, never take a dime of child support, survive and raise me."

Married at eighteen, Ahsha's own marriage ended when her two children were young, only one and three. "I didn't want my kids growing up in an argumentative, dysfunctional house and thinking that kind of environment is normal," she says. She admits that leaving was hard and painful, but she did what she thought was right. And now she can see the blessings that have come out of the pain—including her newfound faith in God and relationship with Christ.

Sometimes you don't know how much you want something until it's taken away. Ahsha was not brought up going to church, but she wanted to go. Her husband was Catholic, so they married in the Catholic church. She went to the required classes and learned a lot about God, but "I didn't have a relationship the way I do now. I didn't start finding that relationship with Jesus until going through my divorce," explains Ahsha.

But even before she had a relationship with Jesus Christ, she somehow knew that taking her kids to church was something worth fighting for. "When you're young, you have this idealism of what you're going to do when you're married, and I wanted to go to church on Sunday. And then it didn't happen. I remember one time we had even talked about going the night before. I woke up. I got both kids ready. He was still sleeping. He said, 'I'm tired. Let's not go.' I wasn't strong enough in my faith, or myself, to go without him. I was following his lead."

When they divorced, however, her husband included in the divorce decree that the children must be raised in the Catholic church.

"At the time, I didn't think much of it," said Ahsha. "I would pick up the kids from his house on Sunday night and take them to church because he wouldn't take them." But eventually, as Ahsha started to attend a Lutheran church, she began taking the kids with her instead of attending two different churches each Sunday.

When her ex-husband found out, he reacted angrily. Ahsha recalls, "He said I was in contempt of court. He filed a motion. My attorney told me I couldn't take them to the Lutheran church until the court proceeding was over because the police could put me in jail. Then I had to tell my kids. They were crushed. They asked, 'What do you mean? We've been going (for a while), and we like it there. Why is dad doing this? He doesn't even take us to church.'"

"It was definitely a time of spiritual growth for me," remembers Ahsha. "I couldn't believe a judge was going to show up on my front porch and tell me, 'You can't take your kids to the Lutheran church.' Church and state don't mix for a reason." Ahsha refrained from taking her kids to her church but fought the provision in the divorce settlement. "We both spent a lot of money, and he lost the case. The contempt of court charge was removed, and we changed the papers so the kids could be raised in any Christian religion. It was definitely a trying time."

But in the midst of the conflict, Ahsha's own faith grew.

"I remember I was just tired of it—tired of arguing and fighting. I remember looking out the window of my apartment at that time. I said, 'God, I don't want to do this anymore. Whatever that takes. If I have to leave this world, whatever. I'm done.' It was probably the first time I verbally said something out loud to God."

Now, she measures the success of her parenting on whether or not her children have the same relationship with Christ that she enjoys. "That's my main goal," she says. "Can [your kids] do the dishes? Yes. Can they get a job? Yes. That's standard living 101. But can they survive life without a relationship with Christ? Not just memorize the books of the Bible or retell a Bible story, but really have a relationship. It's something I'm still struggling with: how do you teach that?"

She wants her children to know that "no matter what ups or downs or trials you have in life, God is always walking beside you." She wants them "to have that kind of faith and security because I walked a lot of my life not knowing it."

"I tell my daughter Hannah, 'I feel like my number one responsibility as a parent is for you to know this [truth] and to have a relationship with Jesus. Being an adult, I know how it's helped me, but I also know what I would have done differently if I had this relationship at a younger age."

She hopes that her children will choose to embrace their own faith in Christ. She tells of her son Austin being away for a week at church camp, "When I picked him up, he was a changed boy. If I had stayed [in the marriage] where I was, he would not have had that opportunity."

Like most single-parent families, they suffered hard times—eating ramen noodles and hot dogs, living off credit cards, having her van and car seats stolen, and the fighting with her ex-husband (her son says he remembers his childhood mostly by court dates). But Ahsha is still glad she was strong enough to stand up and walk away when she believed it was right.

She recounts as one of her fondest memories the time they spent in their small apartment after the divorce. "It was so simple—just being with the kids and feeling free about it. I wasn't walking on eggshells. I had become so co-dependent, trying not to rock the boat and making sure everyone was happy, that I lost my own identity and sense of self-worth. I remember making dinner one night and thinking, 'Okay, we're in this little apartment, and our life is turned upside down. And things are going to change, but I just feel free. I feel content.'"

35 KELLY DYER FRY—
PLAYING RUSSIAN ROULETTE
WITH ADDICTION

As the editor of the largest newspaper in the state, Kelly Dyer Fry works in a top corner office of a skyscraper with a view of downtown Oklahoma City. There she keeps her favorite picture of her two boys—an adorable candid black and white shot of a two-year-old and a five-year-old playing together in the park.

Perhaps all parents still see their offspring as the children they once were, instead of what they are—especially if they are now heroin addicts.

Not all top executives willingly air their family struggles, but Kelly exposed the details of her excruciating battle against her son Eric's drug and alcohol addiction in an article on the front page of the Mother's Day edition.

Kelly expresses a deep sympathy for other parents struggling to raise their children in much worse circumstances than her own. "When I think that I live in Edmond [a wealthy suburb], my kids went to parochial school, I had lots of friends and family support, and if I could not keep my child off drugs, how does the mom who works two jobs and lives in a rough neighborhood do it? What are her chances? I sympathize for those mothers who are fighting, who have a much bigger battle than I had."

Her son took his first drink at a family wedding at age fifteen and immediately descended into addiction. "It was not the regular thing," she says. "In no time at all, he was gone. He was in rehab by the time he was seventeen." Today, her son—a former high school state finalist debater—is now a twenty-seven-year-old recovering addict. "He is good today," she says of her son Eric. "That's all I ever say. It's chronic. You're fighting it, or it's fighting you."

Her son has told her many times, "Mom, there is nothing you could have done to stop me." Maybe not, but Kelly is convinced that parents can delay exposure to drugs and alcohol and preaches about the dangers of underage drinking. "Scientific research shows that the later drugs and alcohol are introduced into your system, the better chance of avoiding addiction. The teenage brain is still developing. It is so critical to keep drugs and alcohol away from kids during that developmental stage. I think as a society we are too cavalier [about the effects of drugs and alcohol]."

Kelly believes "whole-heartedly" in random home drug testing and maintains that parents are giving their child a "gift" of a convenient excuse to walk away from those offering drugs or alcohol. "Just say to your child, 'You're going to start middle school next month, that's when we start drug testing.' Act like it's nothing. Say, 'That's what we believe in as a family because drugs and alcohol are so dangerous.'"

She has learned from her son's struggle that there is a one in ten chance that a child has the addiction gene. "He is one of those one in ten kids," she says of her son Eric. "Would you let your child play with a ten-chamber gun with one bullet?"

But through it all, she survived by her faith, her strength, and her friends. "Without faith, I don't know how you get through anything," she says. "I don't know how you function. I don't know how you put your feet on the ground in the morning." She says her church and their Catholic school were like her own small town within a big town.

Kelly encourages single parents to cultivate and invest intentionally in relationships outside their immediate family. "When you're a single parent, if you don't have a good network, you're sunk," she says. But she cautions that to maintain that network, you have to give back as well, with carpools or volunteering or babysitting. "You can't slack off and say, 'I can't do that. I'm a single mom.' If you treat yourself like a regular family, then you'll be accepted as a regular family. You really don't have a choice. You have to survive. I think we're all capable of doing more than we think. You find the strength when you don't have a choice."

Kelly also says she believes in angels who gave her strength, but not just ordinary angels. "When I had a particularly stressful day," she says, "I'd envision my angels not as fluffy white cherubim with wings and halos. They were like secret service men who would walk beside me and hold me up. That was very comforting."

Perhaps those angels were off-duty one particularly frustrating morning when Kelly was pulled over by a police officer on her way to school. "It was one of those crazy mornings. My license is stuck. I'm yelling at the kids. I'm trying to get my license. He looks at me and says, 'I'm just going to let you go.' He was afraid of me, and he had a gun! You want to steer away from crazy mothers," she laughs.

Her friends not only helped her through the hard times, but also introduced her to her current husband of seven years. She married "the best person I know" and regrets the ten years she spent worrying "about being alone the rest of my life. I wish my faith would have been stronger. I wish I never would have given that a second thought. It's hard for us to have 'forward-faith.' We all have 'hindsight faith.' We look back at how all the pieces fit together. You just never know what God has in store for you."

Kelly Dyer Fry is the editor of *The Oklahoman*, the largest newspaper in the state of Oklahoma. The story of her struggle with her son's addiction in her own words entitled, "A Thousand Hail Marys to Florida," can still be found on the paper's website at newsok.com/addiction.

36 REBECCA JEAN HARRIS– BEAUTIFUL STONE

"I will show you what it's like when someone comes to me, listens to my teaching, and then follows it...like a person building a house who digs deep and lays the foundation on a solid rock. When the floodwaters rise and break against that house, it stands firm because it is well built." Luke 6:47-48 NLT

Rebecca has spent her life trying not to move. She is one of eighteen people in the world diagnosed with familial inverted choreoathetosis, which causes the muscles in the lower half of her body from the waist down to twist and writhe aimlessly. In other words, her hips and legs are always uncomfortably moving back and forth, much like her family.

"We have moved around so many times. I can't tell you how many houses we have lived in since my divorce in 2004." Abuse, assault, and finances have forced Rebecca and her three sons Donavon, Colin, and Tajammal to move from one place to another for the last ten years. Yet the desire of a house they could call their own still lingered heavily in their hearts. Rebecca says she even named her youngest son, Tajammal, which means "beautiful stone," reminding us that our children are the ones who tether us to the earth; when we are with them, we are home.

So when she had the opportunity to plant their roots, she took it. "I decided it was time to buy a house."

Rebecca's dream home turned into a nightmare. In the first two months, "so many things went wrong. The toilet broke, which caused mold in the bathroom and my middle son's room. Then my oldest son fell through the ceiling in the garage when he went up to clean out all the stuff that was left by the seller." But nothing could have prepared them for what they discovered next.

"I moved the mirror that was still leaning up against the wall from when we moved, [and] I found a pile of what looked like sand, all over the floor." That sand turned out to be a toxic poison which her family had unknowingly breathed in for over two months. "I ended up pretty sick, experiencing bad cold symptoms, feeling like my throat was on fire, and I eventually passed out one morning after taking the kids to school." When she woke up hours later, she called a friend to take her to urgent care.

A doctor diagnosed her with chemical poisoning. "I was told that due to the fact that my house had been poisoned I needed to leave my home and not go back until [the state] did an air filter reading and got a 'zero result.'" Rebecca and her family were homeless for forty-five days.

A certain termite company, (which can't be named because their faulty practices are still under legal investigation) mistakenly pumped large amounts of termite poison into the walls of Rebecca's new home until it pushed up through their floors and into the borders of her sons' rooms. The environment was so unsafe that in order to clean up the mess they "had to put on masks and hazmat-like suits" before entering her home.

After getting the doctor's orders, she and her family were on the move again. Rebecca spent the first few days and all the money she had to put her family into "a hotel close by so that we could have easy access to the kids' schools."

"We then stayed with a few friends, bouncing around from home to home. Finally, the boys and I got tired of all the bouncing and said they would rather sleep in the car than continue to jump from home [to home] every few days." Eventually, "we took the patio furniture cushions (from the backyard) and laid them out (on the floor) in the garage for beds for the boys while I slept in the foldout chair."

During this time Rebecca managed to keep the boys in school, complete the online courses she was taking for her bachelor's degree in organizational leadership, and finish the testing for Tajammal who was diagnosed with ADHD and ODD (Oppositional Defiant Disorder)—all while being homeless. She never let her lack of a house prevent her from creating a home. "I always remember the nights we played UNO or watched movies together, the night we took a marker and drew on each others' faces. Through this whole thing I watched my family bond and stay strong together even when we felt like run[ning] in different directions."

Despite having their lives flipped upside down for forty-fives day, the Harris family's attitude landed right side up. Rebecca says what matters most to her is "keeping that connection" with her children with whom she spends quality time every day. Rebecca even started a home business called DC&T Baked Goods so she could stay at home with her boys, whose names make up the company's initials—DC&T, after Donavon, Colin, and Tajammal.

Although she can't stop moving her body, she will never have to move her family again. "This house is our home."

37 LYNETTE LEONARD –
COMPOUNDING WISDOM

In the corner office on the top floor of an impressive bank known as Allegiance Credit Union, President and CEO Lynette Leonard recalls harder times when she began her journey as a single parent. "So here I am, a young, divorced, single parent. No money. No furnishings. No skills. I had to try to figure out what you can do from there."

With a two-year-old and a newborn in tow, Lynette moved into low income housing and got a job at a little credit union in Shawnee, Oklahoma. "I started as a teller, minimum wage. Your kids need to eat. You've got to find a job. I actually could have made more money if I had stayed at home on welfare, but you have to start somewhere. Money was always a challenge, but I lived on what I had. I didn't do debt."

Financial wisdom is not just her job, but her heritage. "Everyone in my family were either farmers or preachers. There are no harder workers than farmers. My Dad taught me to live within our means."

Lynette credits a long list of mentors, along with her father and her former boss, Gary Parker, who helped her become the woman she is today. "I can never forget my first job at the credit union. This little old professor comes in, and she's talking about how paying a late fee is an absolute waste of your money. All that means is that you didn't plan accordingly. For a single parent who doesn't have any money, why do you want to pay $20 for a late fee when that can be grocery money? I think that made such an impression on me, I can plan."

Lynette began planning, and it wasn't long before her plans for a brighter future became a reality. "I had a good work ethic. I wanted to succeed. I just kept working in different areas of the credit union, kept moving up, and it was a challenge. But you do it, you just do it."

"You are always just going and trying to make it work, especially at the credit union. I remember back in those days we didn't have everything on computers. So if you're trying to balance at the end of the night, you don't leave until everything is balanced. The daycare closed at six, and sometimes I would go get the kids and bring them back to finish. I'd take their sleeping bags, put them under the teller counter, and they would go to sleep. I'm serious. They loved it!"

Lynette's goals were for her kids to be financially self-sufficient, have a sense of purpose, love God, serve others, and be independent. "In fact, when we lived there in Shawnee, we only lived three or four blocks from the credit union. So we had this deal when the kids came in that they got a Dum-Dum, but if they made a deposit, they got a Tootsie Pop. So my daughter, any time she got one dollar, she'd go over and deposit it so she could get her Tootsie Pop! But she learned to save really young."

Her daughter Jaena is now saving money for hundreds of people as CPA and partner at the firm Bledsoe and Associates.

"All of my kids are really smart. They have a good work ethic. We told all of the kids that if they went to college, we would pay half. And if they wanted to go to college, they would have to pay the other half. They could do student loans. They could get good enough grades to get scholarships, or whatever."

From oral surgeon to firefighter, all five of Lynette's children are living proof that you get out of life what you put in. "You just work your way out of it. I think too many people get dependent on others instead of saying, 'Okay, I can take charge of this.' Your kids see that. That's why I think our kids have gone on and been successful. It's that they see how much their parents have had to work to have any success. That becomes a model for them. I wanted to set a standard that my kids could live up to. Even though I started out making so many mistakes, I want them to see that even when they make mistakes they can get past that and do really great things."

Despite all of her success as a career woman and a mom, Lynette wants other single parents to know that "you are going to make so many mistakes—that's just part of the job." In a world where our identities are often defined by our jobs, our value by our paycheck, and our home by its square footage, Lynette Leonard reminds us that "what's important to your children is not financial. It's knowing you have somebody to count on so that your kids can say, 'I know I have someone who's going be there for me.'"

38 RITA ARAGON–
THE GENERAL

Major General Rita Aragon has true grit. Measuring only five-foot-one, her tiny stature and quick smile belie her iron toughness. The small two-star diamond charm around her neck may imply her rank, but it's her call sign, Paladin, that offers a more accurate picture of this decorated veteran. The airmen under her command nicknamed her after an old television gunslinger often sent in to "clean up the town." They also gave her two pearl-handled six-shooters to go with the name.

She began as an enlisted airman basic and rose through the ranks to become the first female to hold the rank of brigadier general in the Oklahoma National Guard. Along the way, General Aragon also achieved many other firsts—the first female commander of an Air National Guard unit, the first female base commander in Oklahoma, the first female one-star general, and finally the first female two-star general. Now retired from the military, she serves as Oklahoma's first female Secretary of Military and Veterans Affairs, continuing to advocate for the men and women of our military.

But she started her journey in the Air National Guard as a single parent desperately trying to make ends meet. A teacher by training, she struggled as the only breadwinner after a city bus crushed her husband and his motorcycle. The accident left him first physically injured, then his personality permanently changed. He refused to return to work although he was medically cleared, says General Aragon.

He disappeared when she filed for divorce, never paying child support or contacting her or their two young daughters (three and four years of age at the time). Her full-time teaching job brought in only enough to cover her girls' daycare, so she picked up two part-time jobs while trying to finish grad school as well. To say she was stretched to the limit was an understatement. "For three years, I bought absolutely nothing for myself. No underwear. No makeup. We were 'The Three Musketeers.' We went everywhere together," she remembers. She even took her daughters to graduate classes with her, instructing them to color quietly in the back.

One day, an elder in her church encouraged her to join the Air National Guard. "We'll pay you more than you're getting at McDonalds," he said.

From the start General Aragon distinguished herself from the pack. "I broke the first rule of the military: 'Don't volunteer for anything.' I volunteered for everything! If I didn't, I wouldn't get noticed or get a chance."

Looking back now on an impressive twenty-seven-year, barrier-breaking career including two assignments at the Pentagon, she downplays her achievements. "I'm just a girl from Dale, Oklahoma. I'm not smart. I don't have any special talents. I just took every dirty job that no one else wanted to do, did it to the best of my ability, and I left it in God's hands."

One thing she did better than most was "give as good as she got." While some "cute young things" turned heads with a svelte figure and fresh face, General Aragon got attention by kicking posteriors. After discharging a twenty-eight-year veteran senior master sergeant in her first commanding position for disparaging a female airman, she got a reputation for cleaning house.

In her next post, she cemented her reputation by choosing not to reenlist a master sergeant who intentionally gained weight to avoid undesirable duty. "But everybody loved me who weren't the bad guys," she says, "because it was so nice to have someone who actually followed the rules. You knew what to expect. Ninety percent of the base was loving me, including the commanders, because I was cleaning up all their messes."

Next, she was chosen to command an aeromedical evacuation squadron facing their Operation Readiness Inspection (ORI). The 150 medical personnel were so undertrained and under-promoted, they were in danger of failing. In one week, General Aragon brought in the training and cut through the bureaucratic red tape that had held up promotions for fifty personnel. And despite the special challenge of melding the part-time Guard with the full-time military, Aragon successfully built an esprit de corps that earned the unit a rare "Outstanding" review on their ORI.

She encouraged a spirit of teamwork and took pains to foster respect for enlisted personnel. She would tell officers who felt it was the enlisted's job to cater to them, "You got that backwards. Officers take care of the enlisted. They are the ones between you and death."

And that was only the beginning. To list all of the highlights and honors of General Aragon's remarkable life and illustrious career would take a book, but thanks to her part-time schedule, she still made it to sporting events and home for dinner each night with her girls while they were living at home.

Feisty and tough, but warm and fun-loving as well, General Aragon has inspired the love and affection of those around her throughout her career. At her enormous retirement party her well-wishers raised $14,000 ($25 per person) to donate to the National Women's Memorial in her honor.

And surprisingly, she credits her extraordinary leadership ability with her twenty-two years of experience of working with children. Serving in the Air National Guard allowed her to continue her career in education along with her military career. And she received similar accolades in that career—

honored first as an Oklahoma City Public Schools Excellent Educator and then as Principal of the Year. "I know how to build a team because I played with little children—giving them confidence in themselves, teaching them that they are an integral part," she says.

What started as a desperate measure by a single mom to save her children has transformed not only General Aragon and her family, but countless others in her home state and around the world who have benefitted from her leadership.

But she doesn't take the credit. "Faith is a big part in my life—always has been, always will be. When I was a kid, I used to pray, 'Make me relevant in this world, help me be something that spreads goodness and makes things happen.' I have no doubt that all these wonderful things in my life are because of that faith."

A partial list of General Aragon's many honors and achievements include the *Journal Record's* Woman of the Year, the *Journal Record's* 50 Making a Difference, the Oklahoma Women's Hall of Fame, Oklahoma Woman Veteran of the Year, Tulsa Women In Communication's Woman of the Year, and Single Parent Support Network 2013 Legacy Award Winner.

photo by Stacey Zahn Photography

39 GLORIA HUDSON— WISDOM FROM THE WOMAN AT THE WELL

Gloria Hudson thinks that God might have included the story about Jesus and the woman at the well in the Bible just to comfort single moms. "No one ever sets out to be married five times and end up single," she says.

In the story of the woman at the well, Jesus breaks social convention and overcomes our human predisposition to judgment when he asks the woman for a drink. He reveals he knows her sins (having been married five times and living with a man who was not her husband), but offers her acceptance and love in the form of "living water," which if she drinks, she will never thirst again.

Gloria can relate.

She has traveled the rockiest of roads having her five marriages shattered one after another by infidelity, by domestic violence, by abuse of her

169

children by their stepfather, and finally by her husband's death after a seven-year battle with cancer. "My lack of discernment was a horrible curse and hurt the ones I loved the most," she says. Yet through it all, she (and the Lord, she is quick to add) managed to raise two beautiful, successful daughters who even nicknamed her "The Fun Queen" for her positive, cheerful outlook and approach to all the storms life threw at them.

"Sometimes, I'm amazed," she says, "I can't believe the resilience of my daughters. They are both college-educated, driven, incredible mothers, and good cooks who give back to their communities."

She has good reason to be proud. Her oldest daughter is the co-founder of a non-profit for children of divorce and has authored two children's books to help children navigate and overcome the hurt of divorce. Her youngest daughter attended graduate school at Boston University and is an accomplished woman in the business world.

But Gloria also has what all parent's desire even more than their children's success—her children's admiration and respect. "I will never forget," she recalls as she tells the story of when she was introduced to her youngest daughter's sorority friends. Her daughter said, "Guys, now listen to my mother. She is very wise."

Gloria willingly shares her hard-gained pearls of wisdom, "I understand the pain of divorce. It feels like a fresh wound. You try to make sense out of what happened. You are scared and just lost part of your identity. But wounds can heal if properly treated. I can't change my past, but I am willing to share pearls I collected along the way from the sandstorms in my life."

As many other veteran single parents do, Gloria speaks of the need for forgiveness, the danger of bitterness, and the hurt caused by the almost irresistible urge to disparage the other parent, "Sometimes we act like wounded animals lashing out. Children are often the recipients of this abuse. But saying hurtful things about a child's parent also affects the child's own identity."

"I would bite my tongue in two before I would ever say one bad thing about my children's fathers," she emphasizes. "[The children] absorb everything like a sponge."

"Extend forgiveness to the ex-spouse whom you've felt rejected by," she encourages single parents. "This will build a healthy foundation for raising content children. If a parent feels rejected, they may develop a victim mentality and function as one rejected, so everyone can see how badly they were treated. Children often model their parent's behavior. They become angry, distrustful, bitter, resentful, or rebel against authority. At the least, they will experience conflict because they need and love both parents. Bitterness destroys lives."

Gloria also warns against a common tendency for parents to cave in to their children because of guilt from the divorce. "Children need boundaries. Boundaries provide security. A lack of boundaries can cause a child to become self-centered and rule the household. They need strong boundaries of love, support, and encouragement."

Everyone's situation is unique, but Gloria offers three key factors that worked for her as a single parent: consistency, communication, and confidence creators.

"Consistency is critical to keeping children calm during crisis. We tried to live in the same house, attend the same church, keep the same friends, the same teachers, to keep continuity."

"Communication with your kids is so important whether you are married or single," she adds. "Listen. Take what they tell you, and use it to guide them." She tells of talking with her girls about sexually-active friends or other issues they confronted. "I didn't act shocked. I just said, 'Pay attention to what happens to her.' I kept the doors open to talk about any subject."

For example, when her oldest daughter asked her about a close relative being atheist, she responded, "It's funny. If a person lives by biblical principles, he will have a happier life. Is your uncle happy?"

"No, he's anxious all the time," her daughter quickly replied.

"The realization was a turning point for her," said Gloria.

Gloria believes that we shouldn't spend so much time listening to what other people say about God, but rather developing a relationship with Him for ourselves. "I told my kids, 'It's up to you to decide what you believe.' I know God is real. I can see clearly now His love and hand on me at all times, protecting me and my daughters, always taking care of us."

Finally, she recommends the importance of helping your child find their niche or finding "confidence creators." "Children need multiple opportunities to develop skill sets, make friends, and discover themselves," she says. "Activities such as sports, drama, debate, dance, leadership, and art help to create confidence—confidence that will pour over into other areas when a child masters something."

Gloria recalls watching her oldest play basketball. "I loved going to games," she remembers. "I couldn't stay in my seat." She was amazed at the changes in her daughter once she found where she excelled. Her new confidence even helped her to succeed in areas where she had previously failed. "Once children find their niche, it becomes a springboard for future success. We believe in our children, and then they believe in themselves."

"A lot of kids want to give up when they don't feel good at something. We have to let them know they are lovable. Think about snotty-nosed little kids; they assume they are lovable. We take that away over the years by speaking negativity."

Not everyone has such an affinity with the woman at the well. Not everyone has experienced such a litany of heartbreak. But for Gloria, just like the woman at the well, unconditional love can turn heartbreak into joy. As Gloria tells her daughters, "I let them know while they had different dads, they have one Father. We all need to be loved by our Father. We start to relax once we know we are loved. He allows us to go through some difficult experiences because we need them to grow. He turns our trash into his treasure. Even though the road to the well was bumpy, I made it to the well and found Jesus, who is able to provide living water that I may never thirst again."

the most important things in *life* aren't things.

photo by Heath Dodd © 2013

40 GINGER A.—
BLESSINGS FROM THE STORM

"You can't be blessed, unless you need a blessing. You can't be a blessing, unless there is someone who needs to be blessed. Whichever one you are, allow yourself to be."

--Doug Bradley, Oklahoma native and multiple tornado survivor

Trapped underneath the pile of rubble that used to be her home, Ginger A. twisted her arm in pain to make the only call she could—to her parents.

She left a message, "Mom, I'm trapped in my house."

Now safe after the devastating F5 tornado that ripped through Moore, Oklahoma and destroyed Ginger's home along with hundreds of others, Ginger says of her desperate phone call, "I knew that even if police were keeping everyone else out, no one would be able to keep my dad from coming to find me."

Heath Dodd captured the photo above of the rubble in Moore only hours after the storm destroyed over 1300 homes on May 20, 2013.

Thankfully, her father didn't have to pull his own daughter out of the wreckage of her home. Using every muscle she had, Ginger was able to dig her way out and was taken to a safe location. Because of the chaos and limited phone coverage caused by the disaster, however, she was unable to communicate to them that she was safe. Fearing the worst, her parents did indeed press their way through the secured perimeter and past the acres of devastation to dig through the remains of her home for an hour with her oldest son Johnathan (nineteen) before they finally received the good news that she was alive and safe.

Twenty-four other Oklahoma families that day were not so fortunate.

Only days on the other side of losing everything she owned to the largest tornado in American history, Ginger doesn't talk about loss, she talks about blessings. "All of my past trauma of house fire, divorce, etc. have long ago released me from the strings of material possessions. I have let it go. I have my kids. I have my friends. It is true, if you have friends and family, you can get through anything, especially if you believe in the strong hand of God."

But she still wonders, "Why? What purpose? Why was my life spared? Why do I feel blessed in this trial more than I feel cursed? The faithfulness of God has calmed the storm within my heart even though the world around me has collapsed."

When Ginger first knew the tornado was headed her way, like most parents, her first thought was of her children's safety. She rushed to the high school to try to get her two children, Steven (seventeen) and Joanna (fifteen), but the tornado sirens were sounding, the school was already locked down, and the staff wouldn't release them—an ominous sign considering that the tornado narrowly missed the high school and later hit two elementary schools in the same area injuring dozens and killing seven third graders who had taken shelter in a hallway.

As Ginger raced home to take cover herself, she drove parallel to the giant grey funnel tearing apart everything in its path. She entered her house, stood in the hallway, and called a friend. Then, the tornado struck. She managed to crawl toward the bathroom as debris fell all around until she was finally buried, unable to move, except to make that one call letting her parents know she was trapped.

But the miracle of her survival amidst a pile of rubble was only the beginning, as Ginger experienced the outpouring of love and God's provision from those around her in her time of need. She recounts with wonder, "So many blessings and miracles...not in the form of monetary but in the form of physical, tangible miracles. The givers have given. The encouragers have encouraged. The prayer warriors have prayed. And Oklahomans have been Oklahomans."

Thousands rushed to help storm victims in the wake of the overwhelming destruction, but as Ginger noted, "It is difficult to walk into a room of volunteers and realize I have nothing except what they give me. I have my clothes and my children. I have insurance that will barely meet my needs."

But in the midst of her trial, she sees a perfect picture of God's love, "You must be willing to receive. God has been faithful to send givers. In order for a gift to be received you must be willing to accept it. What a perfect analogy. We are given eternal life and salvation but the gift goes unclaimed if you do not accept it. No one can force you to take the charity bestowed upon you in times of trouble, just as God cannot force you to receive his gift of life."

She also sees a picture of what she wants her life to be, "We are the feet and hands and heart of Christ. Our service to others is what God intended His church to be. To give is to be blessed. I had to come to the place where I would be willing to receive so others could be blessed in giving."

Ginger, who is no stranger to trial having experienced a bitter divorce and losing her previous home to fire says, "All my past trials have prepared me for this—the greatest trial of all. Faithful church goer I long ago ceased to be; believer I have always been."

"But the outpouring of love and care and encouragement upon me has lifted me up to new levels of spiritual awareness. I pray for strength knowing God has always proved himself faithful before."

"What have I done to deserve these blessings? Nothing! But He has given them anyway. Why did I live? It was not my time to go. I do not understand, but I want to say, 'Here I am, Lord. There are people who are hurting, and I have met the Comforter. Bless me, bless me, so I can in return bless others!'"

41 ROY PAGE—
SAY WHAT YOU NEED TO SAY

Roy Page spent decades building a fairy tale life with his wife and their two children. Then, in 2009, in what he calls "a perfect storm" he watched their dream ripped apart—with the failure of his twenty-year marriage, the erosion of his successful business in the wake of a national recession, the death of his revered father, and potentially life-changing surgery for his beloved son—all in the space of less than two months.

In his upcoming book, *A Letter to Evan: An Average Dad's Journey of Discovery and Discernment Through Divorce,* Roy leads by example in sharing his heart and soul with his teenage son—and with fathers everywhere struggling to regain equilibrium and maintain their role as fathers in the aftermath of divorce. Below is an excerpted chapter used with permission (©2013 Roy Page, published by Lucid Books).

"Hold Nothing Back"
by Roy Page

You and I both like John Mayer. I still hate we missed that concert. ... One of Mayer's songs is titled "Say." It is among my favorites. The lyrics state: "Say what you need to say, say what you need to say." (Refrain) "...have no fear for giving in. Have no fear for giving over. You better know that in the end, it's better to say too much, than never to say what you need to say again."

When I wrote this letter to Evan, I felt it could be my last chance to communicate my feelings, love, direction, and affirmation to him. I was afraid Joan might convince Evan I was to blame for all of our heartache. She could portray me as an evil liar. I was afraid Evan's ears would become deaf to me. I felt a desperation, an urgency to put all of my words out there at once before the opportunity vanished forever.

My fears have proved unfounded. I underestimated Joan. I underestimated Evan.

I did not overestimate the great need for a father to express himself to his son. As my friends and acquaintances learned about the letter and the book, I began to hear their stories. I learned the desire of fathers to connect with their children is widespread across age groups, married, divorced, traveling fathers, and dads who are home every night.

I reconnected with an old friend when he emailed to congratulate me on [my company] Third Degree's new Durham, North Carolina office. Over the years he has achieved a level of business success many can only hope or dream to reach. He worked hard and worked smart and earned his success. Many people have ridden his coattails, and most would love to walk in his shoes.

Years ago I entered into a business relationship with him and his company. It didn't go well. It didn't end well. We parted ways and never communicated again, until the email. I immediately responded. Moments after I clicked send my office phone rang.

He was surprised to learn Joan and I had divorced. Soon he shared how events of his life had kept him from letting people get too close. These barriers caused him to lose many people who were once close. He expressed pain of our failed friendship and business relationship. I interrupted mid-sentence to tell him he didn't need to ask for my forgiveness. He said, "Roy, please let me say this. I need to say this to you."

He continued while I listened, then I also shared my pain. I confessed to competing against him. I've grown past the desires of one-up-manship. I expressed that I no longer wanted to compete against the people who mean so much to me.

My long lost friend's timing was a blessing that day. We said what we needed to say and then we talked about our kids. His were growing up and branching out into their own lives. His son and daughter were both in college, one all the way in Scotland. I told him about writing this book and the letter to Evan that was the impetus for the project and a large part of my personal healing.

After emailing him a copy of the letter along with the introduction to the book, he was inspired to reach out to each of his children by writing them a letter. I hope he does that many times.

Recently I've witnessed a trend among the fathers who work for me. These young men in their twenties and thirties are part of the "dad blogger" movement that is strengthening across America. They share stories and say what they need to say about being fathers. This type of sharing leaves a great legacy and diary of their lives for their children to read someday. Their blog posts are often about time spent with their children. Perhaps the desire to find material for posts encourages them to spend more time with their children. It's a great movement, and I'm learning from them. I enjoy seeing the enthusiasm and pride they take in fatherhood and their children.

My time with Evan is more limited than that of the typical "dad blogger" of younger children. Though I can't recapture lost time, I can make the time we have meaningful, enjoyable, and fulfilling, and I can continue to offer and invite him into my life.

I make the same effort with [my daughter] Kendall. She and I recently played golf with another father and daughter.

We had a great time together on the course. We were doing something fun and just enjoying each other's company. Near the end of our round, my friend said, "Roy, I don't think I've ever seen you and Kendall this close." The deepening of our relationship was apparent. I attribute that to the purposeful time we have spent together. She loves it when I am completely engaged in our conversations, absorbing the details of her life I've missed since seeing her last, when I am participating in activities I know she enjoys, and including her in activities I enjoy. Our time together is intentional, meaningful, and comforting.

I'm a much better dad now than I was in my last five years in the marital home. I've become a completely different person. My kids reap the benefits of my self-improvements in the overnights, the longer visits I have with them, and when they accept my invitations of extra time. When we're together, we're together. It's just us. That feels pretty good to me, and I hope to them.

Kendall has asked me many questions over the last three years. "Daddy, do you still love Mommy?" "Why does Bubba not come over to spend the night with us?" "What happened to you and Mommy?"

I'm sure she has had just as many questions for Joan. At the age of twelve she sees and she wonders.

I love Joan, and I miss her. I miss the marriage we once had, and I'm sorry it couldn't be saved. During one of our counseling sessions while legally separated, I said things that hurt Joan. For a moment it felt good to finally say what I needed to say, but soon afterwards I became disoriented with feelings of regret and guilt.

I contacted our counselor to ask for a private meeting. I needed to speak freely and openly to gain a sense of perspective on what I was feeling. I needed to be in a safe environment. I told our counselor I was struggling with the comments I had made. Our counselor quickly pointed out, "Roy, you said what you needed to say and what she needed to hear. She said some hurtful things to you as well."

Unfortunately, Joan and I could never get past the words and find common ground from which to try and repair, rebuild, and rewrite our fairy tale. We share the blame and responsibility for that.

Words are powerful. They have been known to start wars, fuel a movement, be written and remembered through the passage of time. Why would the same not be true in a marriage or other personal or business relationship? Once spoken, words can't be erased, only remembered.

In business I write a script for what I want to say during a sales presentation, and often it is rehearsed. When producing a television or radio commercial at Third Degree, we draft a script and storyboard to ensure we are saying what we mean to say on behalf of a client's product or service.

The client can change it and we can renegotiate the script, but it's used to clarify what will be said. In my marriage I needed a script that I never wrote, but a marriage is not a business relationship; it's an emotional relationship. I wish I had been more prepared to say what I meant to say. Saying what you mean to say can be risky when you are out of practice. Feelings and emotions suppressed and kept in a dark closet for a long period of time recoil at the harsh light of exposure. The longer these emotions are hidden away, the more painful they become when exposed. I've learned the importance of communicating early and often.

Life with Evan is different than we thought it would be. Evan and I shared a few days of his spring break together in North Carolina. There was no little sister and no Mom. It was just the two of us. We spent time looking out over Oriental Harbor at the sailboats moored behind the rock jetty, the same we've seen for the past three summers.

We watched the shrimp boats being prepared for the upcoming season with shrimping captains hopeful for higher prices after the 2011 oil spill in the Gulf of Mexico. We fished together, landing a few speckled trout, then grilled our catch to perfection. We enjoyed time skipping across the chop of the Neuse River in our seventeen-foot Boston Whaler. Evan had no complaints about waking up before noon. Anticipation of the day was his alarm clock. Evan didn't say much during our time together. He didn't need to talk a lot. Just being present with him said all I wanted to say. Perhaps he felt the same.

With Evan, I am careful about what I say. I know he will remember my written and spoken words. He will carry them through the passage of time. It is my hope and prayer that Evan will tuck my letter away in a safe place, and when he feels the need to hear my words, he will take it out, read it and reflect on it. I hope he will call to ask me what I meant by the words. We will have a great conversation.

42 TROYVONNE HAMILTON— JOSIAH MEANS JEHOVAH HELPS

Most mothers can tell you the date their child was born, but Troyvonne Hamilton is the kind of mom who can tell you the day of the week. "Josiah was born on Wednesday, September 28, 2005. My baby is my life. I live and breathe Josiah. I tell people that he is the reason I exist. I was born to be a mom. I absolutely love being a mother. I can't even explain the joy that I get when I'm taking care of my son!"

Taking care of Josiah means starting her day at 3 a.m., when Troyvonne wakes up to give him his first of four doses of medicine. The second dose will come after breakfast when the food Troyvonne prepares is pureed and fed to him. For the rest of the day Troyvonne will feed, change, medicate, and transfer her son, via wheelchair, in and out of their van as they visit one of any four therapists in different states. At night, she will hook him up to his oxygen machine, connect a gastro-intestinal tube to his side so that he can receive life-giving nutrients in his sleep, and attach his body to a medical monitor measuring his stats—all because the medical staff at his birth hospital chose not to treat Josiah for jaundice.

Josiah has kernicterus a preventable brain injury caused when newborn jaundice goes untreated. "No doctor wanted to label him kernicterus because that should not happen to any newborn," says Troyvonne. After a two-year struggle she finally got the diagnosis. The hospital's mistake left Josiah with permanent brain damage and this terminal illness. Her son is bright, but his body keeps him from talking, walking, and doing normal daily activities.

You can't put a dollar amount on a person's life. However, you *can* put a dollar amount on how much it would have cost to save Josiah's: one dollar. "It's a $1.00 test (for jaundice). One dollar can save a baby's life." With the help of her mother, Troyvonne is working to pass Josiah's Bill. "The law would require every newborn in the state of Oklahoma to be tested for jaundice before they leave the hospital." In 2008, Senate bill 1645 passed through the Oklahoma State Senate, but was rejected in committee. Troyvonne and her parents vow to keep working to get the bill reintroduced and passed so no children in Oklahoma will develop kernicterus. "You have to do something; no child should have to suffer a very preventable brain injury. We can't just sit there and do nothing."

Troyvonne is always doing something between working to get her bachelor's degree, single-handedly caring for her special needs child by doing the job of a full-time nurse, caring for her son as a single parent making her a full-time mom, and fighting the legal system on behalf of all babies born with jaundice. You may wonder where she finds the energy to keep going, but Troyvonne knows. "Josiah taught me to fight. I am going to keep fighting for him because I saw him fighting in the hospital for his life." Now "I fight for him."

Troyvonne fights to help others, but when it comes to helping Josiah she says emphatically, "No! I don't help him, he helps me. Josiah has brought me closer to God. I know that He has a plan and a purpose for Josiah and myself. We have gone through a lot, but it has all been a learning experience for Josiah and for me."

"I'm learning from Josiah about everything around me, about life and why

I'm here. I've gone through all of this so that God can use me according to His purpose and His plan, and He's using Josiah, too. When people come into contact with him, they see God's spirit and the love that God has just flows off of my son, and it draws people closer to Him. You see Josiah in a wheelchair and you see a beautiful little boy, happy, always smiling, and you think: my life can't even be as bad as I try to make it out to be."

Though Josiah's time on this earth is uncertain, neither he nor his mom are bitter. After undergoing baclofen pump surgery a few months ago, Josiah slipped into a coma for over a month heightening Troyvonne's appreciation for whatever time she has with her son. "He was in ICU, and he wouldn't wake up. I prayed and prayed, and I said, 'God, I'm not ready for this yet. I am not ready. I need more time with my child.' Right then, He granted my prayer. Immediately, Josiah woke up at 3 o'clock in the morning. He just woke up."

"You see, Jesus comes at 3 o'clock in the morning, or 4 o'clock in the morning, or in the middle of the night. He will come by the grace of God. I have been blessed so greatly, and I am so grateful that God has allowed me a second chance to spend time with my baby. We don't worry about death because death is just part of life; it is not the end. I know that there is a heaven, and there is a hell. Even if my physical body is not here, and Josiah's physical body is not here, we will be reunited one day in heaven. So we are just thankful for the times that we have."

"We are all spiritual beings having an earthly experience. We are just here for a short time. While we are here, we have to do what our plan is and our purpose is, but we will have to be with God or the devil one day. This is not my home. It is not Josiah's home. It is not your home. I know that my eternity will be spent somewhere else and so will Josiah's. He doesn't walk now, but he is going to run in heaven."

ACKNOWLEDGEMENTS

The title of this section should be "commend-ments" because to acknowledge all of the people who helped make this book a reality simply isn't enough. We want to commend you. Scratch that. We want to praise you, or rather, shout your names from the mountaintops so the world can hear of your greatness. But due to the lack of mountains in Oklahoma, we will whisper your names from the pages of this book instead, hoping to fan the flames of your hearts as you have warmed ours throughout the process of writing this book.

To Rhonda Thomas, the director of the Single Parent Support Network, you are a visionary. You turned your idea into a book so that you could continue to do what you do best, helping single parents. We are so grateful for you and all of the good people who are working behind the scenes at SPSN: Barbie, Alexis, Kevin, Bryan, and Christy Johnson.

This book would be incoherent if not for the gifted skills of our editors who took our words and transformed them from alphabet soup to poetic prose, you are the real geniuses. Thank you Cyndy Harvey, Micah Holmes, and Tom Leydorf for donating your time and tremendous talents toward making this book the best it could be.

Our beautiful book cover was designed by the award-winning graphic designer, Kristina Phillips, whose time and efforts were donated to us as a gift because she believed in our cause and yours, single-parent families.

Of course we could not forget the men who shouted *our* names from the mountaintops—of laundry, dishes, and homework—so that we could spend months chasing dreams to change the world through the power of written word. Thank you, Tom and Lou, our marriages to you are the greatest accomplishments of all.

Finally, thank you, God. We felt your presence every step of the way. We saw you not just show up, but show off by providing every need, answering every prayer, and connecting every person to this book whom you wanted in it. You are the real star of this book, the truest celebrity, and the greatest single parent we have had the honor of getting to know. We love you, we thank you, and we pray we honored you through this book. We couldn't have done it without you.

"But those who trust in the LORD will find new strength. They will soar high on wings like eagles." Isaiah 40:31a (NLT)

Sincerely,

Christy Stewart and Micah Leydorf

ABOUT THE AUTHORS

Micah Leydorf (right) is a former Congressional press secretary and deputy chief of staff who gave up politics after ten years on Capitol Hill to concentrate on more important things—namely her family. She now lives with her husband and two sons in Oklahoma. Her move from Washington, D.C. to Oklahoma has given her ample opportunity to invest in family, church, and writing. Micah holds a master's degree in journalism from the University of Oklahoma. While she has spent her life and career writing in many different capacities, this is her first book.

Christy Stewart (left) lives in Moore, Oklahoma with her husband, Louis Stewart. She is a teacher, author, and mother of three beautiful kids: Destiny, Moses, and Hannah. Her job as a freelance writer offers her the freedom to travel the world doing her most important job, supporting her husband. As the wife of an Air Force officer, she has felt first-hand the pressures of single parenting as he travels around the world protecting this great nation we call home.